THE PLACEMAKER'S GUIDE TO BUILDING COMMUNITY

With Best wishes,

Nabeel.

19/10/ '10.

D1477135

THE PLACEMAKER'S GUIDE TO BUILDING COMMUNITY

Nabeel Hamdi

publishing for a sustainable future

London • Washington, DC

First published in 2010 by Earthscan

Earthscan Ltd, Dunstan House, 14a St Cross Street, London EC1N 8XA, UK
Earthscan LLC, 1616 P Street, NW, Washington, DC 20036, USA
Earthscan publishes in association with the International Institute for Environment and Development

For more information on Earthscan publications, see www.earthscan.co.uk or write to earthinfo@earthscan.co.uk

ISBN: 978-1-84407-802-8 hardback
       978-1-84407-803-5 paperback

Typeset by JS Typesetting Ltd, Porthcawl, Mid Glamorgan
Cover design by Ryan Anderson and Rob Watts

A catalogue record for this book is available from the British Library

Library of Congress Cataloging-in-Publication Data

Hamdi, Nabeel.
  The placemakers' guide to building community : planning, design and placemaking in practice / Nabeel Hamdi.
     p. cm.
  Includes bibliographical references and index.
  ISBN 978-1-84407-802-8 (hbk. : alk. paper) – ISBN 978-1-84407-803-5 (pbk.
: alk. paper) 1. Community development–Developing countries. 2. Economic development–Developing countries. 3. Human settlements–Developing countries. 4. City planning–Developing countries. I. Title.
  HN981.C6H364 2010
  720.1'03–dc22

2010000819

At Earthscan we strive to minimize our environmental impacts and carbon footprint through reducing waste, recycling and offsetting our CO_2 emissions, including those created through publication of this book. For more details of our environmental policy, see www.earthscan.co.uk.

This book was printed in the UK by TJ International, an ISO 14001 accredited company. The paper used is FSC certified and the inks are vegetable based.

Mixed Sources
Product group from well-managed forests and other controlled sources
www.fsc.org   Cert no. SGS-COC-2482
FSC   © 1996 Forest Stewardship Council

This one is for Max, and his sister Layla

'Whichever way you go, go with all your heart.'

Confucius

Nabeel Hamdi qualified at the Architectural Association in London in 1968. He worked for the Greater London Council between 1969 and 1978, where his award-wining housing projects established his reputation in participatory design and planning. From 1981 to 1990 he was Assistant, and then Associate Professor of Housing at Massachusetts Institute of Technology where he was later awarded a Ford International Career Development Professorship.

In 1997 Nabeel won the UN-Habitat Scroll of Honour for his work on Community Action Planning. He founded the Masters Course in Development Practice at Oxford Brookes University in 1992, which was awarded the Queen's Anniversary Prize for Higher and Further Education in 2001. He was awarded an Honorary Doctorate from the University of Pretoria, South Africa, in 2008. He was ARUP Fellow at the University of Cape Town and an Adjunct Professor at The National University of Technology, Trondhiem, Norway. He is currently Professor Emmeritus at Oxford Brookes University and Teaching Fellow at the Development Planning Unit, University College London.

Nabeel has consulted on housing, participatory action planning and on the upgrading of slums in cities to all major international development agencies, and to charities and non-government organizations worldwide. He is the author of *Small Change* (Earthscan, 2004), *Housing without Houses* (IT Publications, 1995), co-author of Making Micro Plans (IT Publications, 1988) and *Action Planning for Cities* (John Wiley, 1997), and editor of the collected volumes *Educating for Real* (IT Publications, 1996) and *Urban Futures* (IT Publications, 2005).

CONTENTS

ACKNOWLEDGEMENTS

Thanks to all those who have contributed to the content, structure and style of this book – to keeping a check on clarity of thought and to ensuring (as far as possible!) a jargon-free read.

In particular, thanks to all the students whose ideas I have tapped throughout – I hope I have given enough credit where it is due. And to Supitcha Tovivich (Nong) who has been my teaching assistant at Oxford Brookes University and at the Development Planning Unit, UCL, and to Sara Freys at the DPU. Our studios together generated the wealth of example of student work that illustrates this book. Thanks equally to David Sanderson, Anshu Sharma, Rumana Kabir, Mansoor Ali and Charles Parrack for their insights from practice; to Gabriel and Peter Townsend, my residential editorial team who checked for logic, offered editorial advice, as well as ideas for titles. Thanks especially to Ryan Anderson for originating the cover design and for his tolerance of endless tweaks in colour and form.

Much of the content is drawn from my more recent interviews and discussions in fieldwork in India, Sri Lanka, Ecuador, Peru, South Africa and Thailand. I thank everyone in those countries, colleagues and families in the community for their time and resources. Especially in this respect, to K.A. Jayaratne (Jaya) whom I have known and occasionally worked with since the days of the Million Houses Programme in Sri Lanka and who now heads the NGO Sevenatha. As always, he opened doors and made introductions to all kinds of local organizations, including the Women's Bank.

Much gratitude to Hans Skotte and Ragnhild Lund of the Norwegian University of Science and Technology in Trondheim and to the Norwegian Research Council for the opportunity to engage with post-tsunami research in Sri Lanka and to collect stories and project examples which I have used in Part 1.

I am very grateful to the work of ASF-UK and in particular to Melissa Kinnear and Jeni Burrell with whom I have been working for some years. Our summer schools at The Eden Project and ASF's international workshops have provided me with resources and examples with which I have illustrated method throughout this book.

Two important people to thank: Rachel, my wife, for giving me 'space' to write this book and for all the corrections to the text and advice on illustrations and design. Her support has been unmatchable throughout.

Last, but never least, is Vivien Walker, probably the only one who can read and make sense of my handwriting. Her editorial commentary on theory and method give clarity to the text throughout. On Chapter 8, for example, she had concluded (unfortunately for me) that my discussion on PEAS was somewhat processed! Her advice on phraseology was equally perceptive: holding 'private functions in the community space attached to the public latrines' may just be misunderstood!

Acronyms and Abbreviations

AA	Architectural Association
ACHR	Asian Coalition for Housing Rights
ACP	African, Caribbean and Pacific
ASF	Architecture Sans Frontières
BUDD	Building and Urban Design in Development
CABE	Commission for Architecture and the Built Environment
CAP	Community Action Planning
CASE	Community Architects for Shelter and Environment
CAT	Centre for Alternative Technology
CBO	Community-Based Organization
CDC	Community Development Council
CENDEP	Centre for Development and Emergency Practice
CEO	Chief Executive Officer
DfID	Department for International Development
DPU	Development Planning Unit
EU	European Union
FEDUP	South African Federation of the Urban Poor
GDP	Gross Domestic Product
GLC	Greater London Council
GNP	Gross National Product
GOPP	General Office of Physical Planning
HOST	HOme STay
IDS	Institute of Development Studies
IIED	International Institute for Environment and Development
IMF	International Monetary Fund
INTRAC	International NGO Training and Research Centre
JB	Jeni Burnell
MDG	Millennium Development Goals
MIT	Massachusetts Institute of Technology

NATO	North Atlantic Treaty Organization
NGO	Non Government Organization
NH	Nabeel Hamdi
NHDA	National Housing Development Authority
NSDF	National Slum Dwellers Federation
ODA	Overseas Development Administration
PEAS	Providing, Enabling, Adapting, Sustaining
PRA	Participatory Rapid Appraisal
PRSP	Poverty Reduction Strategy Paper
PSSHAK	Primary Systems Support Housing and Assembly Kits
RDP	Reconstruction and Development Program
RH	Rachel Hamdi
RISD	Rhode Island School of Design
RRA	Rapid Rural Appraisal
RTC	Responding to Conflict
RUC	Royal Ulster Constabulary
SAP	Strategic Action Planning
SEWA	Self-employed Women's Association
SPARC	Society for the Promotion of Area Resource Centre
ST	Supitcha Tovivich
UCL	University College London
UMP	Urban Management Programmes
UNCHS	United Nations Centre for Human Settlements
UNICEF	United Nations International Children's Emergency Fund
WTO	World Trade Organization

PROLOGUE

February 1970 – Bedford Square, London: Nick and I sat in Ching's Yard, the student cafe at the Architectural Association (AA). We were rehearsing the final details of a presentation we were to make to Anthony Greenwood, the then Minister of Housing in the UK, and others. We were to present one idea for an adaptable and socially more responsive approach to housing, based on the work of John Habraken, which Nick and I had worked up as a part of our final year project as students. The phone rang, diverted randomly from reception and equally randomly, I picked it up. It was Ken Campbell, Head of Greater London Council's Housing Division (architects), wondering if it was too late to confirm his attendance, apologizing for his last minute response. I extended to him a warm invitation on behalf of the AA. We would welcome his observations and his feedback. There were some 15 people who had been invited to the presentation and the dinner after, from industry and from local government, including the Minister. It had all been orchestrated by John Starling, our tutor at the time, and his friend Monty Berman, director of Form International. Both had been enthusiastic about the idea and thought it was timely to try it all out.

We started our presentation with a critique of convention, which is by now familiar. Dwelling is a process, not a thing to be mass produced. As local government, you can cultivate the opportunity and provide the circumstances needed to create dwelling, but you cannot make dwelling for people you don't know. Existing methods for providing houses, based on averages derived from user needs research had been notoriously bad at meeting the needs of anyone in particular. Our existing housing was difficult to adapt to meet the needs of individual families or the changing needs of public authorities because it was 'tight fit' in standards and other specifications. The housing stock would be unable to continue to provide an economic and socially functional life, as circumstances and aspirations would change, and ever more rapidly.

Habraken's theory, which we had adopted, was simple: instead of building houses, build 'support structures' within which people can make their own houses. How much structure you provided and in what form was negotiable and would depend significantly on the social and political circumstances of place and time. The support would be as if a chessboard, liberating in its range of choice and yet within limits agreed by all in the interests of the collective good. For the local authority, the structure could be parcelled off into a variety of dwelling types and sizes when finished and which could be easily changed to meet the demands of waiting lists.

There was nothing intrinsically new about the idea of adaptability.[1] In Britain, the Ministry of Housing and Local Government had developed an adaptable house, shown at the Ideal Home Exhibition in 1962. The Smithsons were proposing their 'Appliance House' in 1958. In Switzerland, there was 'System 4D', standard frames with flexible interiors. In Sweden there was a variety of projects: in Gothenburg in 1956, in Orminge in 1967, Tensta in 1970, among others – all exploring technologies that would be flexible to users. In France as early as the 1940s Jean Prouve was exploring 'shells and infills', which were easily transportable and adaptable.

What was new this time was that one of the largest public housing authorities in the world, at the time, the Greater London Council (GLC), was listening, and that architects were at last beginning to realize that they were in a position of social responsibility. People would need to participate as guardians of the quality of housing and the built environment, which up until then had been the domain of architects, housing managers and other experts.

The complexities of Habraken's simple idea and the change it would demand in the design and provision of housing and in the roles and responsibilities of experts were significant and reflected in the questions and discussions that followed our presentation: how would standards of quality for design be maintained? How would planning approval be decided, since densities based on habitable rooms would remain uncertain until after consultations with families? Tenants would need to be identified well in advance of completion so that discussion on needs and decisions on design could be made – how would this be done? And what about second tenancies? What if the original layout of the house was unacceptable to the new tenants? How much management would it take to adapt the dwelling to new needs? What, in any case, was the life cycle cost of doing all this?

And then there would be significant changes in relationships, between architects and families, between families and the local authority, between the local authority and the building industry, between contractors (who would build the support) and sub-contractors (who would install interiors).

As chance would have it, it was Ken Campbell who decided to take it on at the GLC and try it out. What followed was eight years of experimentation and prototype development and two pilot projects built in London, the first at Stamford Hill, the second at Adelaide Road in Camden.[2] While the first was limited in what it was able to achieve, given all the constraints, the second at Adelaide Road went further. We were to develop a range of tools with which to engage families – models, tenants 'design-it-yourself' manuals, computer programmes to help families decide on layouts, all of which were novel at the time. At Adelaide Road, after the first meeting with families (unprecedented in its own right) each would get a manual with the envelope of their dwelling on plan. Each would take time to sketch out their ideas. During the months that followed, I would receive phone calls during 'surgery' hours at the GLC – families wanting advice or reassurance: would it be practical to do this or that.

As the support structure was building we (architects, housing managers and component suppliers) set up an office on site with a large model and met with each family to test ideas and make sure it would all work and to budget. Then we would step out into the empty structure and chalk it all out to get a sense of scale. Families would meet and exchange ideas and socialize – a sense of community and belonging began to develop well before occupation.

And throughout, there were negotiations with housing manage-ment on standards and the limits of acceptability of ideas; with the Ministry on subsidies and the planning authority on densities and standards and then again with families on constraints, mediating the needs of all without losing the trust of any or the essence of the ideals we were working toward.

In their post-occupancy review of Primary Systems Support Housing and Assembly Kits (PSSHAK) in 1980, as the ideas became known, Alison Ravetz and Jim Low talked to many of the families, 18 months on.[3] There were, for example, the Goulds (mother and daughter) whose needs were moderate and yet made nonsense of the standard house plans. They wanted two separate bedrooms in their two-person flat. 'Officialdom does not accept that there are people who wish to share a flat but not a bedroom.' Others had been reluctant to get fully involved and found the process difficult. 'I found the drawing of plans most difficult. Getting the most out of the space without waste ... for a person like myself it was hard to visualize the completed flat, for when I saw the walls in position it was not what I quite intended.' Others embraced the process throughout: 'We as a family, took the planning seriously, spending hours thinking about it and working things out to what we thought would be to our best advantage.' 'I found making the plans very exciting and made Photostat copies of the plan and got all my friends to help me in designing my flat ... my class of children at school, who were 10 years old, also wanted to be involved and designed all kinds of flats...'

From these early beginnings with participatory work and with adaptability, five themes emerged, well known now yet still troublesome, which have carried through into my teaching and progressively into my work in international development:

- The knowledge that participation is not something you tag on if you have the time or good will, but an integral part of making design and planning efficient and effective. It underpins today's concepts of partnerships and good governance. It cultivates ownership and, with it, a sense of belonging and responsibility, both of which are important to the health of place and of community.
- That change is integral to assuring good fit between people and place over time. Places grow, adapt, transform in response to needs and circumstances, if allowed to do so and, if not, become a burden on the economy and on people who become captive in the absence of choice. The social consequences are by now well known. How should we cultivate change?

- Participation and change put experts in a very different relationship to people and to place. The changing roles and responsibilities of experts, providing skills and scoping out opportunity, enabling others to imagine the future that begins now, cultivating change and then sustaining it all socially and economically, gives us a very different picture of the expert. This exploration into the nature of our professionalism and how we cultivate the skills and competencies in teaching, demand a progressive process of reflective learning and good communication.
- The forth theme is about the relationship between the structures we design and those that we enable to emerge. This relationship is dynamic and in constant need of adjustment. Structures, by design, offer community a shared context of meaning and a shared sense of purpose and justice, with rules and routines that offer continuity and stability. The question, from those early beginnings, remains: how much structure will be needed before the structure itself inhibits personal freedoms, gets in the way of people and progress? At what point does it disable the natural and organic process of emergence? How much is negotiable and with whom?
- Finally, I have learnt from the earliest days that the best way to tackle the primary constraints that get in the way of change, participation, emergence, whether in standards, cultural norms or legal dictates, is incrementally and with example. The concept of catalyst – of practical interventions with strategic objectives, looking for starting points, building prototypes, is key. In this sense, I have held on to John Turner's axiom and applied it liberally: I know what a house is … but what does it do?

These themes recur throughout this book as we explore the place of placemaking in building community and sustaining human development. We will explore the skills and tools that placemakers need to become effective and responsible Development Practitioners. The book offers insights into the complexities faced by experts when deciding interventions in the informal settlements of anywhere and a rationale for engaging with these complexities in the production of an architecture of opportunity.

I have preferred to use placemaker in my title (rather than architect, planners or experts) because it is inclusive of all who make and sustain the quality of human settlements, including principally the people and communities who are the inhabitants. The intelligence of place, I continue to maintain, is in the streets of places everywhere, not in the planning offices of bureaucracy.

This book is a compilation of my own field notes and lectures, training programmes I have undertaken for non-government organizations (NGOs) in various countries, of student work and reflection, of teaching notes and project evaluations. It is in this sense my own open notebook of ideas and routines as I stumble upon them in teaching and practice. I call it a guide in the hope that it will be informative and useful to others, and who knows, maybe even interesting!

The book is structured in four parts, reflecting my own cycle of work – learning from practice, doing practice, reflecting on both for method and rationale, teaching – from fieldwork to class work, from class work to fieldwork.

In Part 1, Learning From Practice, we build an understanding of themes and issues that always recur and which discipline our work in Part II. We visited a number of places, housing projects provided by governments and charities, upgrading programmes designed with communities, holding camps and squatter settlements. We looked, listened and learnt. We learnt, from failure and success, about the processes adopted for planning and design, and how interventions were decided, by whom and with whom. We learnt about the appropriateness and inappropriateness of standards for layout and houses, about public space and social space, about the resilience and resourcefulness of people, and about all kinds of vulnerability. Why we ask, have lessons that should have been learnt from the early days of mass housing and master planning, still not filtered through effectively into the mainstream of practice?

Part II, Placemaking, is about practice on location. It is about deciding a range of interventions for upgrading on site and building community using a variety of Action Planning methods and toolkits to transform and revitalize a poor urban area. We give definition in practice to participatory work and debate the ideals and techniques of participation with fieldworkers and project teams. Examples in practice demonstrate throughout how small, and sometimes unlikely, interventions when carefully crafted can liberate all kinds of opportunity for enterprise, social productivity and physical improvements. We will see how chance encounters, improvisation, adaptability, can be practical and strategic in building and sustaining well-being.

Part III reflects on the work of Part II and explores more specifically its underlying reasoning and rationale. It explores how practical work can be scaled up and sets out a methodology with which to do so. We see how Community Action Plans (CAPs) can be made integral to Strategic Action Planning (SAP) – both a part of a single project cycle. But it will demand change in expert and agency behaviour and responsibility, and in the process and sequence of work. Each of the components of responsible practice is first outlined: providing, enabling, adapting and sustaining (PEAS). The reasoning and rationale of the CAP/SAP project cycle is subsequently set out; reasoning backwards, I will argue, is a more coherent and equitable way of planning forwards and, at the same time, improves the quality of process and product. I go on to outline a number of key themes of SAP and of scaling up: targeting constraints, learning and communication, reducing dependency, cultivating ownership, reducing vulnerability, building livelihoods.

In Part IV, we turn our attention to teaching and learning. We revisit Parts I, II and III and ask: how do we bring our understanding of practice into the classroom, and in ways that are engaging and fun? How do we avoid oversimplification and encourage the idea that uncertainty is a condition of creative practice, and not a barrier to it? What kind of expert does it take in skills and competencies to converge the mess and creativity of practice with the ideals of development? What does it mean to become a PEAS professional? Teamwork, role play, simulation, negotiation, consensus building, as well as more technical design and planning skills are all explored in relationship to a designated place and country, in a studio in which I have taught over the years at Oxford Brookes University, University

College London (Development Planning Unit) and The Rhode Island School of Design. I illustrate the teaching and learning process and experiences with student work and student commentary.

Finally, we reflect on our work and devise a code of conduct based on what we have seen, heard, done and learnt.

I

THE EVOLUTION OF DEVELOPMENT AND THE PLACEMAKER'S TOOLS

A SHORT INTRODUCTION

'In 1876, King Leopold II said that his goal for Africa was to bring civilization to the only part of this globe where it has not penetrated, to pierce the darkness that envelops entire populations ... a crusade worthy of this age of progress.'[1]

It is hard today to agree with either the goal or motives set out by Leopold. And yet, the concept of bringing civilization (development?) and promoting progress being a crusade (for some) resonates still with some of the ambitions, if not policies, which underpin the politics of aid under the guise of development.

If we look back to more recent history, we will see that the evolution of ideals for international development have witnessed many brave ambitions to bring development to the needy, to generate wealth, improve well-being, reduce or eliminate poverty, to make government and governance more fair, more accountable and transparent, to save the world from climate change and its people from the evil of despots.

In this introductory chapter, I will map my own selective views of the evolution of ideas not as a historian but as a teacher and development practitioner trying to understand where we were in thinking and doing, where we are now and why and what difference it has made to the tools and methods of practice. Specifically, I will do this through the lens of urban development and, in particular, urban housing and settlement planning, perhaps the largest component of any placemaker's task, given all that it encompasses: design, construction, land, infrastructure, tenure, financing, management, participation, governance, partnerships and rights. My purpose here is to introduce a number of key themes that we will explore in more detail, progressively, throughout this book.

URBAN HOUSING AND
URBAN DEVELOPMENT

In the early 1950s and 1960s, the need for reform in housing and urban settlements was largely driven by the desire to build a new Utopia, free of slums and informal settlements. With the growing demand for affordable housing associated with progressive urbanization, you tooled up, scaled up and built up, as high as you could and as densely as you could, according to standards we thought were suitable for everyone in general but no one in particular. Standardization, it was thought, was the key to mass production. If you could reduce it all to numbers, type plans and building components, then you could make it all cheaper and quicker. Everywhere, in cities of countries in the north and south, the demolition of slums and clearance of informal settlements was the norm. 'The values and living conditions of squatter settlements were obstacles to modernization and had to be obliterated.'[2]

In developing countries and under this regime of 'clearance' in pursuit of modernity, informal settlements were seen as an intrusion into the life of cities and the formality of city planning in its search for the city beautiful. They 'were perceived as a manifestation of poverty not an opportunity for urban productivity'.[3] As such, urban growth and urban housing would be strictly regulated in design and production and administratively rationalized. Housing policy was (and still is?) an instrument of political and social reform in response to public health and public strife, rather than benevolence.

It wasn't long, but long enough, before questions were being raised about the effectiveness and cost of these highly centralized processes of planning and production. In the mid-60s, providing a 30 square metre finished house for every poor family would consume

25–50 per cent of gross national product (GNP) in most countries.[4] Those who could afford to spent 3–6 per cent on all forms of shelter, the poorest countries 0.5 per cent. Standards were too high and so, therefore, were costs to the poor, despite the subsidies. Research suggested that those who needed these houses most could not afford even the most highly subsidized rents, particularly because later governments were required to remove subsidies to meet the demands placed on them by structural adjustment.

It soon became apparent that deficits of adequate shelter grow rather than diminish, not just because not enough houses are produced, or because technologies fail, but because expectations rise as housing becomes available; because we did not allow adequately for the reduction in household size; because we failed to count concealed households that come into being as soon as housing becomes available; because more people live as independent households as income rises; because of the unpredicted increase of migration to cities; because of conflict or natural disaster that displaces thousands, many in cities and into cities.

The watershed in the debate on shelter and settlement came, arguably, in 1976 at the UN-Habitat Conference in Vancouver. There was, for the first time, a formal recognition of the informal sector as a legitimate provider of housing and other services. With a little bit of help in credit provision and a few adjustments to standards, a little less in costly regularization, then the informal sector could provide housing and services in a way more acceptable to city planners, more affordable to families and more fitting to the political ideals of how cities should look and function. The question became not how to eradicate but rather, how to incorporate this informality into formal housing.[5]

The principle that emerged was simple. Don't invest in building houses that people can do in any case for themselves and could do better with a bit of help, but rather invest in the collective good that people can't provide for themselves: in land regularization, infrastructure planning, security of tenure, self-build opportunity and credit provision. These themes came together around 'sites and services' and the many forms they would take: open sites, core housing, roof loan schemes.

The World Bank was quick to move sites and services into its own free market ideals. Their lending for sites and services projects in 1972 was partly in response to stopping the growth of informal settlements (rather than incorporating them) and partly inspired by the opportunity to mould self-help into 'its own neo-liberal frameworks which relied on free markets, individualism and payment by users...'[6]

The first World Bank experiment with sites and services in 1972 was in Senegal with 4000 lots in Dakar, the capital, and 1600 plots in Thies. It was the first of a series of projects designed to explore alternative approaches to housing 'which did not rely heavily on the public purse, which mobilized private savings and addressed shelter needs of the city as a whole'.[7]

During the 1970s, World Bank policy had begun to shift away from housing projects and towards urban projects in which housing played a key role. The Bank pursued four linked strategies during the 1970s: urban shelter projects, urban transport, integrated urban projects and regional development projects. These were intended to guide governments toward a '...broader perspective in the urban sector...'[8]

Between 1972 and 1982, the World Bank lent more than two billion dollars to some 36 governments, financing 62 urban projects within the above categories.[9]

By 1990, it had financed 116 projects in 55 countries. The Bank's own review of sites and services projects in 1976 was positive. They were more affordable and, therefore, generally more accessible to the lowest income groups; their impact on improving the socio-economic conditions of the poor was moving in the right direction; and the repayment of loans did not cause negative impacts on household expenditure on food or other basics.

Criticism of sites and services grew, however, as more projects were completed and more evidence was collated. Architects and planners were worried by their technically rational design emphasis, their use of coefficients of efficiency, as the major determinant of design and planning decisions. These projects lacked art. They were ignorant of context and resentful of culture.

Others argued that these projects required the same level of centralized planning as public housing projects, that they displaced people who depended for work on inner city locations, rather than the periphery where most projects were located, that the cost of their administration was high and that they would polarize classes and present far fewer economic opportunities than in the mixed economies of informal settlements.[10] Families would sell out when they had finished building and would return to their shanties. There were few guarantees that people would repay loans, which made them unattractive to private banks: in this sense, the banks targeted people with steady incomes, which most of the poorest do not have. In short, they would fail to reach those in most need unless governments continued their heavy subsidies for land and infrastructure, which they could not afford to sustain.[11]

In the early 1980s, in response partly to the critique of sites and services, partly to increasing housing deficits despite the effort and partly to better understanding of settlements and housing as a social process, not just a unitary one, there was again a significant shift in policy: upgrading or 'integrated development projects' became the focus of shelter and urban development policy, still combining the building of some houses where necessary (for migrant workers, single parent households) with some serviced sites, but primarily concerned with improving the existing stock – first in formal slums and later in informal or squatter settlements.

Instead of making large transfers of money to building projects, the World Bank directed its funds more toward the reform of policies and institutions: to public administration, to local banks and to providing technical assistance. Its terms of reference for borrowers encouraged programmes to be designed more on the basis of effective user demand and less on preconceived notions of adequate housing.

Upgrading was supported widely by the World Bank and others into (and beyond) the 1980s, so that public authorities could 'restore formal control over land subdivision and house building processes, while seeking to mobilize the energies and resources of low-income groups for either the improvement or creation of shelter'.[12]

Most upgrading programmes entailed the provision of loans for housing improvements, sanitation, electricity, water and drainage, the paving of streets and footpaths, the legalization of tenure rights to land (a policy designed to control the growth of illegal settlements) and the provision for improving facilities such as schools, clinics and community centres. Costs had also been reduced, on average to US$38 per household for infrastructure improvement, compared to the many thousands of dollars per household for conventional housing provision.[13] A large number of projects involved regularizing land in order to establish legal boundaries to property (the basis to issuing titles) and to get services into otherwise inaccessible settlements. And most programmes, out of necessity rather than desire, confronted the interests of demands of local residents.

In the early 1990s, and after the usual plethora of conferences and learned papers, we see the beginnings of another significant shift in shelter and urban development policy. It was in response to a variety of findings. Critique of upgrading suggested that many programmes serve only the most able, physically and politically, or the most enterprising; that programmes were often overly 'synchronized', more fitting to the routines of planning than the *ad hoc* arrangement of informality; that the rate of cost recovery was worse than that of sites and services projects and that they had failed to turn the tide of illegal occupations – indeed, in some cases, had encouraged it. Land regularization and the legal titles to land had also fuelled an informal market in land speculation. This, together with the push to recover costs by the local authorities through property taxes, was increasing rents that were forcing the lowest income groups out.

Importantly, the shift in policy came in response to findings that successful programmes had been small in scale, relative to demand and difficult to keep going. They were difficult to sustain because of all the management and administration they entailed over the long term, unlike the one-off projects of earlier years. They were difficult to sustain and scale up, not because of bad design, but because of poor management. What we got was a 'move toward management reform rather than bricks and mortar'.[14]

Urban Management Programmes (UMP) were, essentially, technical support collaborations between United Nations Centre for Human Settlements (UNCHS) and the World Bank.[15] Their focus was on more effective ways of managing land, money, skills, knowledge and other resources, promoting housing and urban development across a range of sectors and at an urban rather than project scale. All of this fitted well with neoliberal policy – eliminating supply constraints to encourage private sector involvement, formal and informal; withdrawal of the state from direct provision to that of enabler; elimination of subsidies to balance the budgets; capacity building across a range of organizations, government, non-government and community based, and exploring new forms of partnership.

The move, in other words, was even further away from site-specific interventions and toward city-wide, market-wide and inter-sectoral programmes. The focus had become more strategic in deciding interventions and increasingly on sustainability and on poverty. This was reflected in a series of global initiatives and proclamations.

For example Agenda 21, adopted by the UN Conference on Environment and Development in 1992, promoted sustainable human settlements. This included tackling social and economic constraints, as well as conservation and management of resources (land, water, etc). Strengthening the role of women, NGOs, the private sector and local authorities, continued as key themes in promoting sustainability.

Then there was the Habitat Agenda, adopted in June 1996 by 170 governments. It had two main objectives: ensuring adequate shelter for all and the sustainable development of the world's urban areas. The talk was of enablement, participation and international cooperation on major social and environmental initiatives in pursuit of sustainability.

In 1999, the World Bank and UN-Habitat founded the Cities Alliance. Their focus was on eradicating urban slums, or at least improving conditions for some one hundred million slum dwellers by 2020.

More recently, there were the Millennium Development Goals agreed in 2000 at the UN and which set out in Goal 7, Target 10 to halve by 2015 the proportion of people without safe drinking water and basic sanitation and Target 11 to achieve by 2020 significant improvement in the lives of at least 100 million slum dwellers. And yet, according to UN statistics, as of recently:

- 840 million people globally are malnourished;
- 6 million children under the age of 5 die every year as a result;
- 1.2 billion people live on less than a dollar a day and half the world's people on less than two dollars a day;
- the income of the richest 1 per cent of people in the world is equal to that of the poorest 57 per cent;
- in the developing world, 91 children out of every 1000 die before their fifth birthday;
- 12 million die annually from lack of water: 1.1 billion do not have access to clean water;
- 40 million people are living with Aids;
- more than 113 million children in the developing world have no basic education: 60 per cent of them are girls.

Poverty, in particular in the growing slums of cities everywhere, sits at the centre of our efforts today, across a broad range of urban policies. Nor is it just the poverty of money, measured as it was in the 1960s and '70s with economic indicators, but the poverty of well-being and opportunity as well of livelihoods. McGillivray and Clarke, in their book *Understanding Human Well-being*[16] offer us an excellent review of the evolution of the dominant meaning and measurement of well-being. During the 1950s, the focus was on economic well-being measured in gross domestic product (GDP) and growth. During the 1960s, economic well-being remained the principal focus, although our means of measuring progress shifted to GDP per capita growth. During the 1970s, as we shall see, the policy emphasise was on 'basic needs'. The means of measurement here was GDP per capita and basic goods and services, including food, water and shelter. In the political climate of the 1980s, the emphasis moved back to economic well-being, with GDP per capita as the principal indicator of progress, but we also witnessed the rise of non-monetary factors – health and literacy, for example. In the 1990s, the focus was firmly on human development capabilities. As we broadened our understanding of the experience of poverty, so new indices and theories were introduced to measure and explain it all.

In 1992/93, the Human Development Index added life expectancy, literacy and a composite of other qualitative indicators. New themes, new policies, new areas of research have emerged and are now central to development work – sustainable livelihoods, the importance of all kinds of assets (tangible and intangible), issues of vulnerability and risk reduction. Housing, for example, is recognized as a social asset, in addition to its market value as commodity. Alternative types of partnerships and organizations are encouraged, in particular for providing credit – the Self-employed Women's Association (SEWA) for example, or the Women's Bank of Sri Lanka – civil society partners who would engage in the governance of housing and social enterprise. Most critically, this focus on poverty, new partnerships and alternative forms of finance '...directly tackles perhaps the three most anti poor phenomena of the modern world: the dominance of finance, the emphasis on consumption, and the prevalence of professionalization'.[17]

The urban poor today are recognized for their resilience and productive capacities, rather than their inadequacies, despite the continued burden of discrimination and disadvantage. As such, disturbing power relations, reducing dependency and exploring interdependency is today as central to the purpose of project planning and delivery and to participatory work as are issues of rights and entitlements. These themes and others we will tackle in more detail, in practice, throughout this book.

For now, however, if we track back to the early days at the top of our diagram (Figure 1.1), we can see how each phase in our short history coincides with the evolution of ideals and policies that were devised in pursuit of development. It also coincides with significant shifts in the tools and methods of placemaking.

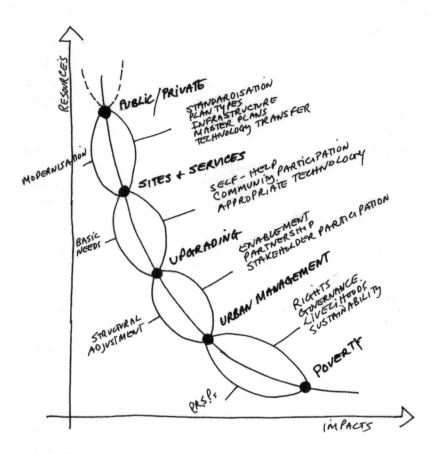

Figure 1.1   *The evolution of development and the placemaker's tools*
Source: Nabeel Hamdi

INTERNATIONAL DEVELOPMENT, AID AND THE PLACEMAKER'S TOOLS

The phase of centralized planning and the public provision of everything including sites and services paralleled, more or less, the 1950s era of modernization. When the ideals of modernization were exported to the developing world they were done so on a simple assumption. If you want to be developed and 'modern' (like us), then do as we do, conform to how we do it in technology and style, use the standards and goals we set ourselves, adopt our vision of a better world and, in time, with a bit of luck and a lot of help (from us) you will achieve modernity!

With modernization came an equivalent set of tools and practices that embodied its ideals and values. There was, of course, the master plan exported everywhere by planners, many trained in the universities of Europe and the USA. The plans were usually explicit about who fits where and how, instruments of control and management – Brazilia, Chandigar, Houseman's Paris, Lutchyn's New Delhi – all models to follow in search of progress and modernity. For housing design, there was the definitive 'type plan' – a distillation of user surveys of likes and dislikes, designed as they were to find the generic solution rather than meet specific needs. Then there was the focus on infrastructure design and all the tools and techniques that came with the planning of sites and services comprehensively laid out in Caminos and Goethert's *Urbanization Primer*.[18] To make it all work technologies were transferred across the world, as was the know-how and expertise of system building and prefabrication, so that it could all be mass produced. It all 'offered [planners] a cleaner slate than any that had gone before. It offered architects the chance to design their way out of the mess (as they saw it) of the organically evolved city.'[19] It enabled both professions to grow and dominate the landscape and the vernacular over people.

The two phases of sites and services and upgrading coincided with that phase in development referred to as 'Basic Needs'. Attention in development policy shifted to ensuring minimum provisions to meet the basic needs of developing countries and their poor, decided in consultation with those whose needs were most urgent. Water, food, sanitation, shelter were explicitly targeted, as we have already seen.

For the practice of placemaking and the tools of placemakers, there were equivalent significant differences. Self-help, working with families and communities on building or improving, was a key vehicle for the design and implementation of programmes. Community participation (the one referred to as tyranny rather than transformation) became a common theme to most placemaking. With it we witnessed an industry of guidebooks and self-help manuals on how to build or improve or adapt, how to install water, sewage lines or make bricks or roof tiles. We favoured structure plans in place of master plans – more open, more inclusive of difference and change, easier to adapt. And instead of technology transfer, which favoured suppliers rather than users, we moved on to 'appropriate technologies', those which were more readily available and sustainable locally.

Upgrading and the urban management programmes corresponded with Structural Adjustment, promoted principally through the International Monetary Fund (IMF). With the debt crisis of the mid 1980s, with shrinking public expenditure as a result and with banks drawing in their outstanding loans, governments were required to reduce subsidies and balance their books as a condition of bank lending. Food, education, health and social spending were mostly targeted. The results in many cases were socially regressive. In Mexico, the percentage of births attended by medics fell from 94 in 1983 to 45 in 1988. In Ghana, there was an 80 per cent decrease in spending on health. In Egypt, there were bread riots when subsidies on bread were removed. 'In Sri Lanka, childhood mortality rose substantially when food subsidies were withdrawn.'[20]

During a similar period, new themes and terms entered the jargon of Development Practice: enablement, partnerships, development cooperation. The sceptics recalled, with reason, the days when cooperation was used as an instrument of world hegemony, an instrument of nations in charge to engineer change in their own interests. 'This struggle for world hegemony was and continues to be at the core of what is lovingly referred to as development cooperation',[21] a process in which 'the poor (and their governments) had to be willing to cooperate' if they were to reap the benefits of globalization and the good life. The results: most who participated became co-opted into systems of production and trade, agreed internationally and reflected in such policies as structural adjustment. 'In practice, the highest toll (of structural adjustment programmes) fell on the poorest social group, not on governments or other elites. Women, responsible for day-to-day survival and for the children, shouldered the greatest burden.'[22]

The language of participation also shifted from community to stakeholder, encouraging all who had a stake in projects and programmes to cooperate in the delivery and management of housing, utilities and services, all of which demanded new skills and routines and a new repertoire of tools: negotiation skills, for example, and conflict resolution, the stakeholder analysis and risk assessment. Planning For Real – a pack of tools and techniques with which to engage with communities, sort out problems and prioritize needs – came into currency. It was first used in Glasgow experimentally in 1977 and more widely from the start of the 1980s. Then there was Participatory Rapid Appraisal (PRA), introduced in the early 1980s, which gained widespread popularity during the 1990s. A whole raft of tools was developed at the Institute of Development Studies (IDS) under its rubric including mapping, transect walking, diagramming and more. Many of these tools and techniques were progressively incorporated into Community Action Planning, an action science-based approach to design and planning, which was pioneered in Sri Lanka in 1984 with the National Housing Development Authority, which in the early days included a team of researchers, including me, from the Massachusetts Institute of Technology (MIT).[23]

It started with government adopting a 'support based policy' to urban housing and settlement improvement, rather than providing public housing as it had done previously. Enablement took on the mantra of political enablement, creating political space for new ideals and opening opportunities for communities to engage directly with government in deciding how best to proceed and in managing upgrading programmes. Land regularization or 'blocking-out' was done with communities and community contracts were issued for the construction of infrastructure. A continuous and adaptive process was set in motion, avoiding the one-off project approach.

The focus throughout, in what became known as the Million Houses Programme, was on community development, on the social agenda integral to the upgrading process. Later Community Development Councils (CDCs) were formalized as partners in the process. They would work with the National Housing Development Authority (NHDA) to identify and supervise construction work. At government level, the Housing and Community Development Committee was established to oversee the process. Housing loan packages were developed, tailored to the needs of individual families, as well as numerous guidelines for their disbursement and management. A Housing Information Service offered families and communities a range of practical tools on budgeting, construction and on organizing and managing contracts. Standards for upgrading projects under the Million Houses Programme were adjusted to suit needs and budgets and specific building codes were developed that would be affordable, appropriate and easy to upgrade.

All of these initiatives overlap into the current phases of urban management and the targeting of effort directly on poverty reduction, as an objective in its own right. Poverty and the effective management of urban and global resources coincides today with the Poverty Reduction Strategy Papers (PRSP) and the Poverty Reduction Growth Facility, a loan fund managed by the IMF.

In its 2001 report on conditionality, the IMF signalled four key changes: stronger national ownership involving borrowers more centrally in programme formulations; fewer conditions attached to aid; more programmes tailored to the specific needs of borrowers; more clarity in the exact terms of compliance.[24] Throughout, the private sector or market enablement would continue to play a key role despite the new language of partnerships and governance. 'A 2006 study of 20 countries receiving World Bank and IMF loans found privatisation was a condition of 18 – an increase on previous years.'[25] The emphasis throughout, in any case, is on aid effectiveness and better coordination of effort.

Two themes are current in this respect. The first is aid alignment and the second aid harmonization.[26] These themes were first debated in 2002 in Monterey at the UN Summit on Financing for Development where donors agreed to increase both the volume and effectiveness of aid; then in 2003 in Rome at the High Level Forum on Harmonization and more recently in Paris in March 2005 in what is known as the Paris Declaration. In Paris, the Tanzanian Minister of Finance said, 'If implemented [the Paris Declaration] will … reduce bureaucratic hurdles, the cost of aid delivery, irrational conditionality, endless meetings, and the misuse of high level talents in recipient countries through aid related meetings, visits and missions.'[27]

Aid alignment to natural priorities also ensures that each country has the strategic and financial capacity to implement its plans. It is about strengthening capacity, making the flow of aid more productive, untying aid where it is still tied. Aid Harmonization calls for donors to coordinate their activities and eliminate duplication, including the coordination of missions and of research and sharing findings – which invokes again the need for cooperation.

> *In 1990, the UN declared that successful Development requires more effective and more efficient international cooperation. 28 ineffective high level conferences later, in 2003, the Ad Hoc Open Ended Working Group on Integrated and Co-ordinated Implementation and Follow-up to the Outcome of the Major UN Conferences and Summits in Economic and Social Fields – was established. (Its members presumably do without business cards.)*[28]

For Development Practice, another layer of themes and ambitions was added to the already dense vocabulary: rights, entitlement, governance, civil society, sustainability, livelihoods, and vulnerability. The British Department for International Development introduced the Sustainable Livelihoods Framework – open to interpretation but an effective tool with which to understand poverty and vulnerability. Increasing urban risks, induced by high densities and the settlement of marginal land in cities, and by conflict and national disaster, today places the emphasis on tools which can effectively manage and reduce risk – on mitigation, preparation and adaptation.

In summary and as we track the evolution of Development and the placemaker's tools we recognize, despite the linear form of the diagram, that each phase is inclusive of others, that the field is layered and networked. As we move, however, from the top of the diagram down, a number of themes emerge that position and give context to practice and to our more detailed discussions throughout this book:

- We note the changing role of the expert, from lead agent to catalyst, from disciplinary work to interdisciplinary work, from producing plans to cultivating opportunity
- We see more participation – away from sweat equity toward empowerment and power-sharing, toward partnership
- The development field is progressively dematerialized from shelter, water at the top, to rights, governance, livelihoods
- We find more integration of disciplines and less sector specific work
- There is more focus on insiders' priorities, notwithstanding the risk, which still prevails, of co-option
- There is more result-based management where gains need to be quantified and progress measured – making aid more efficient, with the use of logical framework analysis
- We see a shift from practical to more strategic work in the desire to tackle root causes of poverty and to scale up programmes
- The Humanitarian Agenda of Rights and Vulnerability is today at the centre of our search for solutions in housing, work and in the management of resources
- We move from a position of providing for the poor to enabling the poor to provide for themselves, recognizing their productive capacities, reducing dependency, building resilience to the shocks and stresses of daily life
- We see a significant shift to urban, in view of the unprecedented growth of urban population and the strain this places on people, on resources and on the environment. 'Cities in the developing world will account for 95 percent of urban expansion over the next two decades and by 2030, four billion people will live in cities – 1.4 billion in slums.'[29]

Where then in all of this is the place of placemaking? What role now for architects, planners and all the other placemakers, experts and non-experts? How do we engage today's agendas in placemaking and, conversely, how does place mediate the demands of these agendas that today make up the business of human development?

PART I
PLACE, TIME AND CLUTTER:
LEARNING FROM PRACTICE

Whatever space and time mean, place and occasion mean more.

Aldo Van Eyck

REFLECTION:
LISTENING TO COMMUNICATE

I was recently in a workshop when I realized that I was not listening, and then I observed that others were not really listening either. Although their body language suggested engagement, they were in fact waiting for others to finish talking so that they could speak.

Good practice hinges on effective communication. A large part of that involves listening, and, importantly, being understood as one who wants to listen. Communication need not always be verbal: plenty of non-verbal communication takes place and, as in the use of tools such as Participatory Rapid Appraisal (PRA), words are sometimes not the main means of communication.

On a field trip to a squatter settlement in South Africa, a colleague experimented with encouraging local residents to draw large plans of their neighbourhood. The purpose of the exercise was to gather information but also to make a connection, in order to learn and share. One man got engaged in the process and soon 'took the pen', drawing streets and building familiar to him, including his own house. The man subsequently took two of us to his house – a modest shack built of tin and wooden crates. Having been invited in, we learnt that the man rented the house that he was a night guard, that he had a girl friend and that he wanted to continue with an education. He told us that his name was July. We also learnt about the local community, about where was safe and where was not.

On another assessment exercise in the Indian State of Tamil Nadu I and team members interacted with coastal fishing communities affected by the tsunami. With a limited number of translators, much of the learning relied on drawing pictures, maps and diagrams, often in the sand. We spent two days with each of two communities and returned at the end to present our findings. Although we were only there for a very short time, we made genuine contact with people, and learnt valuable lessons.

The successful interactions from both of these examples relied on mutual respect and using a body language that reflected this. If people therefore are sitting on the floor, then join them. Actively listen, and avoid reflective sunglasses.

Doing this approach well is about more than mastering tools and their use. It concerns central developmental themes of dignity, and also of partnership, where those with whom we seek to work are not 'beneficiaries' or 'recipients' but are in fact regular people with whom we have the privilege of coming into contact and with whom we have a duty to work with together. Linked to this is Robert Chambers' question, 'whose reality counts?' – the long-term residents of a squatter settlement or village, or of that of the relatively brief visits of developmental practitioners?

Yet, while the importance of interpersonal skills is well known, we (the development practitioners) so often manage to get it wrong. Our ability as 'professionals' to unwittingly patronize seems endless, in our language and in our assumptions. We assume that what we think is what is most important, that we can extract information without consideration of 'giving it back' or of doing much with it.

Part of that is the mysticism with which we surround our own subjects. I think an issue here relates to the degree of fear we have about being wrong and the easy manner of criticism from others who prefer to seek out the gaps rather than to build on what is there.

In programmes we often seem to think we need to know everything before we can do anything. Too many developmental projects flounder under the weight of collecting endless amounts of information, much of which can be redundant, misleading or of insufficient quality. This can be seen all too often in project monitoring and evaluation, where the drive and desire is often to add more and more indicators, in the belief this will make the project more robust. In fact it weakens the project, diverting energies to meeting and measuring indicators, and then debating and refining them, to the point of exhaustion. Clever projects have a small number of meaningful indicators and not a long list. Indeed, such long lists often indicate little more than that the monitoring plan needs more refinement. To these ends the recently published 'Good enough guide'[1] to assessment and monitoring does this, and is a welcome breath of fresh air.

Another area, which I believe is vital for working effectively, is to think more carefully about how we organize what we want to say, and how we do it. Good journalists have the skills of packaging complex information in simple and understandable ways – well-written newspaper articles provide good examples for simplifying the complicated into understandable and usable form.

We sorely lack these skills in development. In teams that are usually multidisciplinary, and often multinational, where a predominant language might not be the 'mother tongue' of all, we do not help our colleagues when we use complex forms of words to describe what in effect can be, on reflection, relatively straightforward. This relates also to use of graphic techniques to explain ideas and concepts. Our sector is too full of overly complex and indecipherable models and diagrams. This does a disservice to the ideas themselves – which might be good, but which are lost in confusing presentation.

To these ends, two maxims, both from architecture, could find more resonance in the work we do. The first is that 'less is more' – in the way that we speak, listen and plan and implement projects, where fewer indicators and outputs are usually good signs, not bad ones, of thoughtful projects. Regarding communicating with people, this may mean listening more, waiting for the gaps and silences, and resisting the temptation to fill them in.

The second maxim is 'to arrive at simplicity' – an instruction that can be applied to the process of assessments, project design, monitoring and in particular the communication of complicated ideas. Simplicity is often confused with being simplistic, when in fact the reverse is true. In fact, staying simple is one of the hardest challenges we face.

David Sanderson

2

THE BAD, THE GOOD AND THE UGLY

Thawra[1] was the kind of informal settlement one sees everywhere: a slum of around 6000 people with no legal tenure, settled temporarily some 20 years ago, along a narrow strip of land adjoining the river and opposite one of the city's prized heritage sites. It was dense with makeshift houses, some well-consolidated, narrow alleys, waterlogged open spaces and not much else, so it seemed. Electricity was mostly pirated from municipal pylons and water was occasionally available through standpipes dispersed randomly with no seeming logic.

Everywhere there were piles of rubbish, some carefully sorted into grades of plastic, card and paper ready to pass on to markets, most decomposing, with pigs and cows and sometimes buffalo grazing wherever, interrupting rickshaws and passers-by. In every corner and on every rooftop, piles of material scavenged from everywhere for building or recycling, buffalo dung patties drying in the sun for fuel, clothes lines and power lines, small shops and workshops – a hive of industry in support of livelihoods and the wider urban economy. And everywhere, in whatever container – buckets, old tyres, oil drums and orange crates, upturned car bumpers and water tanks – were planted herbs and vegetables and other plants, an informal urban agriculture sustaining life and earning money. And everywhere else – enterprise in every conceivable place: in front rooms and back rooms, under stairs and on landings, on roofs, in forecourts, in streets and alleys.

It's worth remembering that between 40 per cent and 60 per cent of cities in the south are made this way, at once productive and vulnerable, a part of the mainstream. In India, for example, in 2002 there were about 52,000 slums in urban areas and nearly 14 per cent of urban households, 8 million people, lived in slums. In Thailand, in 2003, some 5500 low-income urban communities with 8.25 million residents lived in poor quality housing. Three quarters of Angola's urban population lived in informal settlements. In 2002, Dar es Salaam had a population of 2.5 million of whom 70 per cent were living in informal settlements.[2]

In stark contrast to our site, and on the periphery of the city, the latest government attempt to decant and reduce density elsewhere, to settle the latest victims expelled from downtown to make way for 'regeneration' or to accommodate recent migrants flooding into the city. The usual desolate public housing layouts with four- or five-storey walk-ups and public open spaces, all striving for some imagined modernist ideal, resisting it seems, more than accommodating its people. And further still, a variety of charitable projects donated by international NGOs and agencies designed no doubt to best practice, to settle people displaced after conflict or natural disaster.

City-wide, we see all kinds of responses: donor-driven and owner-driven, direct construction, upgrading, self-build, aided self-help and the rest. We wanted, at first, to learn something of the successes and failures of these 'flagship' projects and programmes – the life and death of their informality, of community, of enterprise and organization, and the social life that they had inspired or inhibited. We wanted to see how placemaking makes space for building livelihoods and all kinds of assets, how it might mediate the inequities of income or ethnicity and of fear and insecurity. Given the plethora of experience and book writing, all the conferences, guidebooks and best practice recommendations, you could easily imagine that there was not much more to learn – not much could go wrong! We set off on one of those learning missions to find out, looking and listening, listening and learning. We started city-wide and worked our way back to site.

DAY 1: THE BAD

Our first stop was a housing project recently completed, built by private contractors for the government with international agency money. The layout was typical of anywhere – a series of four- or five-storey walk-ups interspersed with two-storey semi-detached houses. The whole was landscaped with wide streets (in anticipation, no doubt, of the two car per family prediction borrowed from European guidelines for site planning) and the modernist's dream of pavilions in the park, of ample public open space for all, typical of publicly provided housing worldwide.

We looked and listened and measured to learn more about place, about process, about design, about livelihoods and vulnerability, land utilization and the rest. At first glance, few it seemed of all the lessons learnt internationally about good practice had filtered into the cultural practices of agencies and their architects and planners, not least about territoriality and ownership, about public and private space, about identity and belonging. The project had been designed by outsiders, 'maximising their return with considerable technical competence (sometimes) but no intelligence of life'[3] and handed over on completion.

Public open space was there in plenty, uncertain in ownership and intimidating, public and private often separated by the line at your front door, intimidating in its lack of transition.

It all belonged to someone other than the people who lived there although there were signs of appropriation everywhere: bits of rope around one area, used by fishermen to dry and mend nets; a basketball court, fenced and fastidiously maintained by the local club; a tent, serving as a place of prayer in another; an area visible but hedged whose access was hidden, available it turned out, through someone's backyard – itself appropriated for private use. Yet other spaces were claimed subtly by the authority – with 'trip rails' to keep you off the intended green area, or surfaces of sand and gravel that made it difficult to sit or play. And yet others claimed by sponsors with signs that caption 'their aspiration' – a reminder of who it was who gifted it all, who made it possible – Coco Cola Village, Taiwan Love Village, Christian Aid, Friends of Colorado and GAP.

Figure 2.1   *Pavilions in the park: whose identity counts?*
Source: Hans Skotte (top) and Rachel Hamdi

The whole site as a result lacked the social energy and stimulation that comes with density – not the density of numbers so much but rather the density of character and difference, of ideas and relationships that are the social energy and stimulation of place. Instead, we observed people everywhere, sitting or standing, as if spectators 'caught in a strange mixture of fear and fascination ... they dutifully play out roles assigned to them',[4] curious but passive. This 'striving for an ideal perfection rendered the (place) lifeless'.[5] The prosperity of a well-built house, it seems, comes with a sense of solitude rather than belonging.

Inside the houses, we saw private space invaded with a different kind of publicness – the publicness of type plans derived from standards suitable for everyone in general but no one in particular.

Architects, mostly expatriate – the kind of people who search for absolutes, try to get it all 'generically right' – designed all the houses. Mistakes abounded. Some were technical, others reflecting ignorance or misunderstanding or disdain of culture and habit. Standards for design, it seemed, had been borrowed from some social housing guidebook in Europe and adapted, grudgingly, to fit: 6.5 square metres for a single bedroom, 12.5 metres for a double, 3.6 metre widths for living rooms – all arranged on plan with beds, bedside tables, sofas and armchairs!

In one of the flats we walked into we talked to the family about their likes and dislikes of what they had. They complained, as if tenants of a local authority housing project, about things that would not normally have been reason for complaint in their old home. Now that it was all provided, it was the responsibility of others. In the bathroom, a shower unused, in favour of the traditional habit of bucket and bowl. As a result, the bathroom regularly flooded into the hallway. The toilet was broken, the sit-down type and not the more familiar squats. They had climbed on top to squat and had cracked the seat and dislocated the pan from its soil pipe.

Kitchens everywhere were littered with stainless steel sinks and drainers converted to scrub plates for washing clothes more than for draining crockery! A gas cooker stood in one corner – unused. Why, we asked. 'The food tastes different', replied our host, 'and in any case, we cannot afford the gas cylinder.' They had clubbed

"Why, hello darling ... You're home early!"

Figure 2.2   *Standards and Type Plans – generically wrong, ignorant of difference*

Source: unknown

together with a few others in their block and built a makeshift extension for cooking on the ground floor, on public land adjoining the stairwell, with corrugated tin, blue plastic and canvas imprinted with the badge of the donor. This they shared with four other families. Given its convenient location on one of the main access ways into the site, they had set up a few tables and chairs – a small cafe selling tea and snacks cooperatively.

In the early evenings and mornings, smoke from all the cooking and open fires filled the atmosphere, lingering as soot from makeshift stoves and open fires. Designers had failed to consider what at the time was probably a detail in the face of getting enough houses built and quickly: the knock on effects of inappropriate kitchens. We are now learning that 'black carbon' produced significantly from cooking stoves and open fires is responsible for some 18 per cent of the planet's global warming compared with 40 per cent of carbon dioxide.[6] And yet there are, we know, more efficient alternative stoves, more cost-effective for families, which can be locally produced and are friendly to health and the environment.

As we continued our walk, we were shown all around odd bits of unfinished building and poor maintenance. Roofs were leaking because contractors had skimped on materials, reducing the overlap on roof tiles to less than the minimum required to keep the rain out. Doors had already been replaced because they had shrunk and leaked. The lock on the front door had broken and no one would come to fix it. The whole project had been 'handed over' before completion in the rush to meet targets. A strong dependency relationship had been established between families and donors, just as it had been in the old days when it was wrongly believed that building lots of houses quickly and instantly was a good way of solving housing problems.

Before we left, our host showed us a picture of the chief executive officer (CEO) of the agency who had gifted the project. Everyone had got one to hang over their mantelpiece. His portrait smiled knowingly, as if to say 'I have done my job. There may be faults, but you should be so lucky!'

Not far away, an example (Figure 2.3) of what it could look like in a few years with its inappropriate design, inappropriate technologies, without the money and right kind of ownership, nor the institutional care or capacity to maintain or adapt it.

Two streets down, we visited a family living in one of the two-storey semi-detached houses, one of 50 built as a part of 'the estate' to house people displaced after the recent floods. All 50 were similar in type, with some variation in size. Nineteen were donated by Qantas Airlines, 15 by Coco Cola, 17 by GAP and one by Mr Lowes, a kind of philanthropist. Some were empty, families who had stayed back waiting for titles before selling them on. Others were rentals, families using houses as income, now living with relatives in the slums of downtown. Yet others occupied by families not victims

Figure 2.3   *The lost pavilion – occupied, uninhabitable, unsustainable*
Source: Nabeel Hamdi

of the tsunami but there anyway in return for their vote at the next local elections. Some houses had doors and windows missing – but were still occupied. We learnt later that people were selling them on, given their quality, and improvising instead with cardboard and cloth.

The cluster had been designed by architects from Belgium who, in order to 'humanize' the whole and give it character and each house some individuality, had had them painted beige with pink, blue and sometimes purple stripes. It was Walter Segal who back in 1980 said 'to humanise huge structures by architectural means is an unrewarding task … the loss of identity, the divorce from the ground and the collectivization of open space posed dilemmas that cannot be disguised by shape, texture, colour or proportion'.[7]

Outside, by the front door, each house had a tile advertising the name of the sponsor. It all looked modern and could have been anywhere, except where it was. Nowhere else were houses painted this way. It had become known to outsiders as 'the village of stripes', imposing the stigma of beneficiaries, rather than the status of citizenship.

A family of seven told of their discomfort with a house plan that was like everyone else's, not because they were keen on the luxury of style or status but rather because their futures individually needed to be distinguishable, as did their aspirations.

Families routinely consulted their fortune-teller about their horoscopes, which would tell as much about window size and orientation, as about structure and safety. Their discomfort was spiritual, not just functional. In one room, our host pointed to a beam crossing diagonally from one corner to the centre, part of a hipped roof that gave architectural variation outside but which the family considered unsafe inside – a sign of weakness in structure rather than strength of architectural character. They felt vulnerable.

On the far side of the same room, French doors leading to nowhere, the kind that houses 'boast' on estate agents' blurb in Europe. Against these doors, blocking access, was a table offering privacy, security and better use of space. On the table, there was a TV, plastic flowers and colourful dolls. On the wall was a collection of calendars with pictures of obese babies from around the world.

From one of the beams hung a clay pot, filled with silver and other gems – a way of ensuring that the household would not be needy.

Houses were all semi-detached – an unfamiliar relationship to neighbours. Sharing walls, especially inside walls, was like sharing lives. Their walls had voices, they said. Their kitchen, like others, was converted into a bedroom. It lacked the familiar chimney for cooking with firewood, and in any case they needed the space. On the second floor, they showed us their two bedrooms – both converted into classrooms. Their son was a teacher, teaching catch-up maths to late starters.

The family had asked the government for the cash to build their own house but had been turned down. They told of the cost equivalent to US$3000, which they could have halved, and the waste of effort and money. But self-build does not contribute much to GDP, does not generate cash for others, in the same way that contractor-built houses do, especially when the objective of most in government and agencies was to spend, not save.

Among the productive clutter of their outside was a hive of enterprise and industry: chickens and pigs, papaya plants and birds, a fish pond for goldfish for sale.

Of the 250 square metres of house and land, about half was devoted to livelihood-related activities – not something thought about during planning. One family complained that the cluster of houses, as if an island in a sea of public space, did not reflect their 'sense of community and belonging' implicit in their way of life, nor the cooperation of the extended family of relatives and friends, nor their needs. They had been treated as beneficiaries. It was, they said, a process without dignity, despite the generosity of donors. It lacked 'social intelligence' or caring. It was insulting and wasteful. It was all about charity and not about development.

Of the site plan, they said 'we are living together but without community. We talked of our needs but had no say. There is lots of space, but no place to call our own. People here have lots of time, which they cannot fill productively because we are so far from work. And we have lots of clutter, which is now accumulating inside, because outside we are told to keep tidy, in case of inspection. We are, in any case, far from school – a bus ride for our youngest, and some two kilometres walk to the nearest bus stop. Most men spend most of their week downtown on piecework, or back near the coast, fishing.'

The stress, it seemed, on family life was significant.

Despite all the gifts and all the aid, many were still poor – maybe in some ways even poorer. In one woman's own words, 'We still face enormous problems and hardships due to poverty … How to go for medicine for my child with empty hands? The school uniform of my child is torn. I do not have any money in my house to buy a piece of cloth for the uniform. Will she be dropped out from schooling like me? Will it be the same fate for my daughter too? School books? Oh, God! How can I buy these things and continue her schooling? Then milk – food for the small one? Son is dreaming, talking about the educational trip which has been scheduled for next month … From where can we find the money for these things? … More things … More and more things.'[8]

As we left, we noted her signature tile by the front door had been prized off. Her home, she said, had been donated by Christian Aid, but they were not Christians.

Bad design, raised expectations, lack of due process, dependency-inducing behaviour, displacement from community, inappropriate standards, the loss of dignity, the persistence of poverty had all contributed to the stress of daily life and to the malfunction of place, despite the good intent and money. Most people felt abandoned and vulnerable, despite their resilience to cope and survive.

Of the layout, both here and elsewhere we have visited, there was much imitation of northern standards and lifestyles and of old-style modernist ideals, but very little respect or innovation. It was Sennett who said that in order to know *how*, you have to know *where* – which is partly why these projects go wrong.[9] Their *where* was nowhere recognizable *here*. Donor competitiveness, the need to safeguard donor identity, the urgency to dispose of large amounts of money quickly to meet targets, the inexperience of staff in housing, in community developments, in participatory planning, had all undermined the value of place to build community and sustain livelihood.

On our way out we stumbled into the community centre, another gift from some charitable organization. It was a concrete frame building, contractor built, with concrete block infill, all rendered and painted brown, presumably to 'blend in'. Inside four rooms: one office awaiting the arrival of the community development officer yet to be appointed, within a community still fragmented. The second, called the 'theory room' was ambiguous at best in purpose. Then the third, full of computers, was locked should anyone enter until a supervisor was appointed. The last was labelled 'multi-purpose'. All the furniture and finishing was clean and pristine, uninviting to the needs of fishermen or carpenters or all the other enterprises crammed into the 'Parker Morris' type flats and houses.

When later we talked to several of the expatriate project managers, they admitted their lack of experience prior to their presence here, or indeed the experience of their agencies in housing. One had been a teacher, another a social services officer and yet another the manager of a supermarket back home.

Lessons

At the end of the first day, we had confirmed lessons we had thought that we had already learnt, but not it seems in the places we had visited this first day.

We have learnt that belonging is not just about location but about meaning and association – the kind that offer a multiplicity of opportunity for social exchange (cafe), informal encounters in transit (streets) and collective ownership (squares, courtyards), for example. For that reason, we can be at home in different places despite our location. It is common for people displaced, for whatever reason, to belong elsewhere from where they now live. We have also learnt that place attachment can both enhance our sense of belonging and can also act as a constraint, limiting people's ambitions to network social relations city-wide, access markets and break down place associated stereotypes.[10] In this sense where people now live in the public housing site provided confirms their alienation from the every day and the familiar – their sense of not belonging. People we talked to expressed their anxiety about every day encounters with people they didn't know. The result, often, is the constant stress of uncertainty and instability, and the constant desire for elsewhere.

We know that public and private in the context of our project is more nuanced than the planners of our case study would have us believe. 'The public/private opposition suggests seams between worlds that in our everyday experiences are often seamless. There is pretence to clarity where there is opacity... divisions where there is overlap, and a suggestion of simplicity where there is mostly complexity.' 'Realities of city life play havoc with neat divisions. Elegant models of urban life and sharp opposition deployed in their construction may give a lot of intellectual satisfaction to the theory-builders, but little practical guidance to the urban planner and even less support to the urban dwellers struggling with challenges of city living.'[11]

We had learned that placemaking could mediate the interests and values, cultural norms and religious practices of all the different and sometimes conflicting kinds of community we find in place: communities of interest, culture, practice and resistance. Engaging these groups as partners through participatory planning would be as if to 'dance with conflict' both literally and metaphorically, to acknowledge their role as agents of change. In this sense, settlement or resettlement is not just about effective and creative planning, but about community building and peace-building as well. In a project in which there had been no chance of dialogue or participation in design or planning through which differences can be understood and mobilized (rather than normalized) the risk of violence and the perception of insecurity was high and already in evidence, signalled by the walls and barriers and colours and claims and barred-up windows – much as it is in the so-called 'sink estate' anywhere.

Then there are lessons about land utilization. We have learnt that the overabundance of public land undermines the tax base of local authorities, becomes a repository for garbage and winds up a burden for everyone. There are lessons learned based on the numerous case studies collected and analysed by Caminos and Goethert[12] over many years confirming the importance of differentiating between major lines of access and secondary ones, so that responsibility for maintenance and ownership can be clearly distinguishable and standards of construction and treatment differentiated. We saw little differentiation in lot sizes, reflecting the potential for commercial use given the location, nor reflecting differences in use patterns, given all the home-based enterprise on which most will rely for income.

We have learnt everywhere that standards of layout and construction must be flexibly applied and indeed developed and negotiated with communities; that plans must be resilient to 'free or variable or unpredictable behaviour'; that people build at different rates to meet needs and budget; that settlement takes years to consolidate and cannot be instantly provided according to blueprints, despite timetables or the need to satisfy donors. But we also know that all these lessons – all the knowledge and information that we have gleaned from years of experience, of success and mistakes – will only give us a partial understanding of questions that need answers, problems that will need defining again and conflict that will need to be resolved, every time we start. How will land be allocated, how will it be designated and who will decide? What level of utilities should be provided and with whom? Who will manage it given our understanding of good governance? What size lots? What technology will be appropriate and how to reconcile the climatic and resource efficiency of the vernacular with the pervasive desire among people for modernity or progress? What kind and how many houses should be built, by whom and with whom? What hierarchy of circulation will be provided and where will it run? Are there opportunities for partnership, for enterprise – is there space for income generating activities for human development? How will change and adaptation be cultivated rather than interrupted by lack of due care?

For all these questions, we can usually foresee conflicts of interest, conflicts in priority and power relations, conflict in taste and aspiration. Creative design and plans can reconcile some of these conflicts and differences, but never all of them – however much participation we engage in, however many stakeholder analyses we do. 'Good neighbourhood plans have elements of exact surveying, engineering, forecasting and cost, but they are also works of art and politics – or at their best, perhaps works of love and justice.'[13] They are, 'a commitment to truthfulness',[14] a willingness to accept the value and meaning that may modify logic or rationality as we proceed – all of that are crafted technically, socially and artistically. This kind of learning and craft demands openness rather than defensiveness among designers – a willingness to improve our knowledge and skills, and like the craftsmen, to 'learn from touch ... engaging with difficulties, accidents, constraints ... rather than striving for perfection'.[15] Improvisation we have learnt is the users' craft. Improvisers do follow rules, rules of economy and association derived in concert with place and with people. But improvisers adapt the rules and make up their own, a process of progressive fine-tuning to ensure good fit between people and place.

DAY 2: THE GOOD

The following day, I wanted to visit an upgrading project I had worked on some years back – one of many that had started as a slum and since consolidated into a functioning and integrated urban neighbourhood. It was in most respects a success story, not just in process but also in outcome. Of interest to us all was how it got going but, more importantly, how it grew and kept going when typically public and international interests had waned. Equally important was how lessons and impacts had extended to elsewhere in the city and nationwide. How had the process and our interventions delivered the practical goods and services on the ground, while creating space for longer term and more strategic development?

It had all started with the usual community action planning process – intensely participatory, small in scale, problem based and driven by opportunities one finds and encounters on site and in community.[16] Our assumption, as always, had been that most of the resources we will need for upgrading are probably all in place, if we could only find and then mobilize them all – before we flooded the community with outside money and expertise. We

Figure 2.4   *The quality of place and the intelligence of informality*
Source: Rachel Hamdi (bottom left) and Supitcha Tovivich

would progress quickly but incrementally, where each step would tell us something about the next steps. In other words, we didn't think too much before we started doing and we didn't do too much before we stopped to think about it.

The programme itself was a version of the by now well established routine, illustrated in the schedule below:

- define problems and seek out opportunities;
- set goals and priorities;
- search for options and evaluate trade-offs;
- decide on resources and review constraints;
- decide on catalysts to get things going;

- establish project teams and tasks;
- implement catalysts and monitor progress.

The intent, early on, like any programme that is participatory rather than consultative, was to build a sense of cooperation and ownership around each of the components of upgrading, to look for clusters of relationships and allegiances and political organizations to participate with and search for troublemakers – as well as to determine and prioritize needs. We recognized from the start that social control was a major determinant of success when improving neighbourhoods.

First interventions were typical of most upgrading projects: improve sanitation, manage solid waste efficiently and profitably, ensure security of tenure, reduce the risk of fire, improve most and expand some of the houses, ensure access for small vehicles and for pedestrians, especially since most accesses were virtually impassable after the rains. There were added issues of malnutrition, improving access to pre-natal care, of mosquitoes, lack of employment and vagrancy. Electricity was mostly pirated from nearby pylons or friendly meters and clean water was intermittent at most of the existing standpipes. The stress of it all and the threat of eviction were constant.

Because of the high densities and the need for titles to land, to which the government had agreed, the whole needed 're-blocking' – a process of reducing densities, agreeing lot boundaries and in some case widening access. Some families would have to move and most who did, did so on land made available adjoining the site; in other words, no loss of community. There had been innovation in the way this had all been done. A Community Development Council had been elected – a government initiative to establish civil society representation. They were engaged as partners by the NHDA to work on all aspects of planning and through community contracts and also on construction and management.

Skills training and opportunities for enterprise and partnership were key aspects of all the physical improvements, ensuring the social and economic agenda remained central throughout. The sewage lines had been installed and managed by a community management board, supported with technical help from a local NGO. Partnerships were everywhere. Fire fighting, since fire trucks were unable to access the innermost heart of the settlement, even after re-blocking, became a partnership with women – the 'fire fighters league'. The fire brigade would provide water to the holding tank, which would be managed by the league, in case of fire. They had received training from the brigade in fire fighting and fire prevention, and money to do the work. They had then begun to train others in other communities – a network of small organizations that were integral to the service.

For getting the kids to school, and in the absence of a school bus anywhere near, a fleet of bicycle rickshaws were converted with cabbies to carry some six children each – an idea we borrowed from Chittagong in Bangladesh. The fleet would serve a number of settlements. The conversions were paid for by the Department of Education and the drivers were paid employees – partners to the Local Authority. They reached places that the other school buses could never reach.

For waste management, an arrangement was made with a group of waste pickers, like that in Karachi, with equipment and tools provided by the city's refuse department, a social enterprise of private organizations paid by the council that had also become city-wide. They would sort material on land provided by the city, sell on card and plastics and paper of profitable grades, compost degradable waste and sell this on to garden centres and parks departments around the city. For the rest, in each settlement, they would load up the dumpsters at the edge of the site, in preparation for pick up.

For health, a mobile clinic started here and now roaming other slums city-wide. It was run by paramedics from the communities, trained by the health authorities to diagnose the most recurrent of ailments – of diarrhoeal disease and dysentery, but also offering advice on pre-natal care and referring people on when necessary.

It was all working because there was significant political commitment for it all to do so and because of the energy and ideals of key government officials. It was working because constraints imposed by standards of health and safety and those to innovations in marketing and new partnerships were modified and sometimes abandoned, giving people access to resources and opportunities to meet needs and build hope. It had all gone to scale because the poverty agenda was central to the upgrade – and because of the commitment to tackle some of the root causes of vulnerability: social exclusion, dependency-inducing programmes, ownership, belonging. But all this by now is commonplace. There are excellent examples of success worldwide – not to emulate or replicate but to improve our understanding and our learning of why things work the way they do, not just how and when not. Of particular interest in our example, however, was that this and the many other Community Action Planning programmes city-wide, had cultivated an environment of democracy and of opportunity: it had made space for all kinds of urban and national civil society organizations to emerge, not least for micro credit – the Women's Bank – one of a growing number of No. 1 Women's Development Agencies worldwide. As its founder says, 'The existence of a social democratic atmosphere is of great importance for the practical collective planning and activities of the poor uniting with their own people.'[17]

The next day a small group of us went to visit their head office – still in the same, now less informal, settlement, some 20 years after it had started. It was housed on the second floor of a small, unglamorous building – a couple of rooms for office space, a meeting room, a kitchenette and toilet. We met with the bank's founder, Nandagine Gamagne, with Rupa Manel its national leader and a number of women with varied responsibilities in the bank. They told us their story. [18]

Women's savings groups had been in existence for many years, small 'thrift society' type groups of between 5 and 15 members coming together to save small amounts of money as a basis for loans. They worked independently and without much help. Women would save as little as 10 cents (equivalent) per month and borrow to meet basic needs, food, shelter, medicines and sometimes to learn to read and write. Each group would elect a leader and because of the size of each group, there would be trust and transparency without fuss, without the need for outside experts advising them all in good governance.

There had been hordes of experts coming in and promoting micro credit and income generation but few bothered to talk to the women, to value the skills and know-how they had. The Women's Bank was officially constituted in 1989 with branches in 18 districts city-wide. There were at first three groups of some 5 to 15 members per group, then 7, then 22, 48 and now 6000 groups country-wide and community based with 60,000 members. It attracts about US$7 million worth of savings with over 100 branches. In 2004, the Bank loaned about US$2.5 million to its members – 25 per cent for house building or improvements, toilets, electricity, water and sometimes the acquisition of land – money all saved by the country's poorest women. Recovery is 100 per cent. The Bank's current initiatives have diversified, lending for health centres, the training of nurses, income generating and livelihood activities, legal assistance, life and health insurance, assistance to the victims of natural disaster and to men!

Nandargine was clear that in building the organization of the bank, they had started with the resources they had – with eight members saving about 10 cents each. In the early days, they would work with each savings group to build an understanding of the value of pooling resources – not just of money but of social and human resource capital as well – and how to work together equitably, how to establish some ground rules of engagement. It all had to be practical, he said, despite the fact that all group members knew each other well enough – which sometimes itself got in the way of cooperation. There would be continuous dialogue over priorities and wants – what was legitimate to lend for? There would be discussion on values and on economic benefit and social productivity implicit in cooperating or federating with other groups – securing more participatory forms of governance, bridging social capital between groups, reducing isolation, developing strategic capacities with which to influence change.[19] In all these respects, the bank operated as a micro development agency, insiders advising insiders on value and prudence.

The story of one recipient is revealing:[20]

I as an uneducated youth must earn my living by doing odd jobs like these in the building sites and in markets. Market job was better for me and I continued it as I could earn more as a coolie in the market.

One unfortunate day a bag of brinjal was lost from the lorry I was unloading. Two of us were unloading the stuff from the lorry and my colleague left the market site early before the work was over. However I was suspected for the lost bag. My colleague was not suspected due to his friendship with the owner of the goods. I was taken to police station and was asked to pay the value of the lost bag. I had no way to prove my innocence or to deny my involvement in this theft. The only way of refraining from physical harassment by the police was to pay the value of the lost bag of vegetable. It was [$6] and I paid it to the owner to protect myself from police. I paid this money by pawning my sister in law's gold necklace. Still this is at the pawning centre. This happened in 1997.

By this time I came to know about the non-member groups of Women's Bank for daily earners and joined a group recently hoping to get a loan to do some business on my own. There are eight members in my group. They are newspaper sellers, fishmongers, petty traders etc. All of them are daily earners and can save some small amount of money daily. After my joining the group I began to save (17 cents) a day and I could get the first loan of [$26] after weeks' time when I had saved only [$10].

I went to market and bought vegetables for [$4] and started to sell. I go two times a day around my settlement selling vegetable. I also bought a handcart for [$5] making my total investment [$9] for the new business. And I also could pay off my old debts with the balance money. Now I feel I am relieved.

I want to improve this vegetable business. I have two ideas to improve this business. One is to buy another hand cart and buy more vegetables to hire another one as an assistant. The other plan is to find a place in the vegetable market to start my own business where I was working as a coolie. I hope to get more loans from my group after repayment of my previous loan to carry on my plans.

In the meantime I thought of joining a class for informal education at the Women's Bank centre to learn how to read and write. I think I must have this ability to be a more competent dealer in the biggest vegetable market here.

Although I knew my group members very well previously as they were living around me I became more familiar with them only after the formation of the group. Now the members of this group meet once a week and discuss the future work of our economic activities. These

meetings have bound us stronger than we were. And also I would say
that all members in this group are only men. I came to know that this
is the only group of men among thousands of women's groups in the
Women's Bank.

I had to wonder if this were an example (see Chapter 3) of breaking
that cycle of poverty and of the intergenerational transfer of inequity
in a highly gender differentiated society.

Organizationally, each group in the Women's Bank has 5 to 15
members. When the group grows to more, another group is formed
and a leader elected, whom the bank then trains. In one city slum,
one such group had started with 16 members, then grew to 53,
then formed another two groups that each again grew in numbers
until now there are 87. Ten such groups go to making up a branch,
each branch has a maximum membership of 80 people. In some
settlements, we were told, 50 per cent of women were involved
in branch activities. Branches are federated into the National
Council of The Women's Bank, which now has a national executive
and an advisory 'board of intellectuals'. The National Executive
Council itself is made up of the elected members from branches.
Branches do not have a 'high-street style' building or shop but meet
wherever, under a tree, in someone's house, but usually in one of
the many community centres located in settlements. The branch,
in other words, is not an entity or place but a network of activities,
accumulating fiscal capital and social capital as well. 'The emphasis
is on members', said Nandansiri, 'not on branches. This avoids the
tendency after success for branches to become self-serving.'

The bank charges 1 per cent interest per month collected by
each group. Some 20 per cent of its earnings go into salaries and
overheads. Membership of the bank is free and via the group, not
the branch, to keep it local. Membership was open to all, except
money lenders and drug dealers. No money is accumulated in assets
or invested through international bonds. 'The money that comes in
goes to where it is needed', said Nandansiri.

The bank is regularly audited at group level, at branch level and
at the centre. Auditors are first trained completing 100 days of
work and an examination, before they qualify. They are themselves

community members – not university graduates – and have, therefore, the interests of the community central to their task. Economic activity and moral accountability were held in equal measure in guidance of their task.

In 2007, Rupa Manell – an early pioneer who had extended the bank's network to rural areas – received a prize from the Women's World Summit Foundation in Washington DC, one of the 14 laureates awarded that year. On the wall of the office in which we sat there is a picture of Rupa proudly receiving her certificate from Hillary Clinton.

Lessons

Before we left, we reflected with our hosts on what could be learnt from their exceptional example of courage and perseverance, and of small practical interventions that have changed the lives of so many of the poor.

First, the whole grew incrementally, small change with a big vision maybe, but not the kind of single vision that dominates local aspiration. It was all going on anyway – the bank built on these small beginnings and gave it strategic importance and value.

Second, the programme was progressively *scaled up* in membership and then *scaled down* in numbers. It grew in size with the contributions of lots of small autonomous units and small activities that also brought about 'improvements in social productivity'. The emergence of the bank was 'reasoned backwards' from the need for credit and the empowerment of women and the activities and behaviour of small groups or 'thrift societies'. It was an emergent organization that had become connected and sophisticated.

Third, the bank and its organization confirmed what we had known all along: that those who manage should also have ownership, because when they do, all kinds of problems are solved and assets accumulated. 'Direct knowledge of the local situation is a powerful force for creating simple and flexible management, but demand that decisions are taken close to the interested population at the local level of administration ... It is at the local level that health, education, sport, culture and other policies can be integrated in dynamic synergies around the quality of life of citizens. It is at the local level that the register of unemployed can be compared with under-utilized resources to create employment policies. It is also at the local level that the various social actors meet each other, allowing partnerships to be formed in the most flexible manner.'[21]

Fourth, we learnt that the progressive scaling down of groups encouraged a sense of interdependency and mutual gain. It was cooperative rather than competitive, building self-reliance and mutual respect. It was not charity.

Fifth, the process itself, in the early days of action planning, cultivated an environment not just to deliver goods and services, but also to make the political and social space so vital for development. It tackled directly some of the primary causes of poverty and of vulnerability, dependency, lack of ownership, discrimination and the absence of choice, the pervasiveness of constraints – standards, regulations, legislation that need adjusting or removing to make things work.

What lessons, we thought, for cities of the north, for breaking the cycle of inequity induced by global financial institutions!

Finally the planning programme as with other action planning programmes shared the following characteristics: it was problem based and opportunity driven, and based on achievable actions; it was intensely participatory, encouraging rapport and partnerships among all stakeholders; it searched for local knowledge, skills and traditional wisdom as a starting point; it was not reliant on complete information or on comprehensive data searches before it got going; its approach in pursuit of its goal to improve lives and livelihoods was incremental, starting small rather than comprehensive or one-off; it searched out starting points rather than end-states and results were quick, visible, and tangible.

DAY 3: THE UGLY

On the periphery of the city, in a remote suburb, we visit one of the ugliest places I have seen, variously called a 'holding camp', 'transit camp' or 'decanting site'. It was distinguishable from other squatter settlements in its isolation and gatedness (it was fenced in) and its regimented organization. And while most squatter settlements will at least be close to sources of employment, markets and other facilities, this was not. It was ugly for what it symbolized as much as for what it was. For anyone who believes that informality is often romanticized for its creative and sometimes quirky innovations in construction and other aspects, a visit here is a stark reminder of the ugly side of poverty and exclusion, however resilient the people. They had all been suspended in time for some ten years now, their transience in evidence everywhere – temporary shacks lined up in endless rows, still unpacked suitcases, the lack of amenity, the absence of hope.

Various groups had moved up here for reasons that offer a window on city politics, on issues of rights and social exclusion and on all kinds of vulnerability, all in one place. Some had been displaced to

Figure 2.5 *A settlement of shacks*
Source: Rachel Hamdi

Figure 2.6   *Streetscape*
Source: Julio Davila

make way for urban regeneration projects in the city centre. Some
of these had been given grants to resettle, but not yet land. Others
were wrangling over compensation: an extended family of father,
mother, aunt and two married children with husbands, wives and
children of their own, eligible for one grant when they felt they
deserved three. Others were illegally occupying public land and
were eligible for nothing.

Another group, and by far the largest in occupation here, had
been evicted from a public housing project, still under construction,
but which they had occupied. They had lived in sight of the project
waiting dutifully for their tenancy papers, so that they could move
in on completion as promised. They had invaded the project after
rumours that their intended homes would go to others better off
in money and political clout. Their eviction was forced, truckloads

Figure 2.7   *SA's Crappiest Toilets!*
Source: Elvis Ka Nyelenzi, *Daily Sun*, Johannesburg, 11 April 2008

of people loaded and then dumped at this camp. They were considered by the authorities as troublemakers, well organized and determined.

On site there was already an informal land market in operation for people drifting in from elsewhere. People would pay two or three times to parties each claiming the authority to approve a new shack. And when you visited the occasional clinic set up at the makeshift community centre you paid some other cartel to jump the queue. All of which serve to pit one person against another, one side of the community against the other. There had been attempts by the authorities at rudimentary improvements, abandoned because of inter-community rivalry and lack of cooperation. Roads, latrines, water – all were in a suspended state of somewhere between repair and disrepair. One man told of his worry about the formal supply of utilities, of electricity and latrines in particular. He and his cartel would lose out as informal providers, where now they earn a healthy living charging for electricity, supplied from illegal connections to mains. They were fighting, therefore, to disrupt the authorities' plans and any attempt at community organizing. In turn the authorities refused to extend supply until 'the community' got organized.

Another group had taken ownership of most of the latrines. Those that had been provided by the authorities, the ones we had visited at least, had had their squat plates smashed or removed. Instead, colonies of latrines had been built by private cartels, each group labelled as if an ad for resort accommodation: 'loo with a view', 'flushing meadows'. Each was locked. For a small fee we could lease a key for one month, three months or six, and become a member of 'flushing meadows'. A sub-market in key rentals had emerged – those with leasehold ownership renting to others. A hierarchy of power relations and dependences had developed, dividing not integrating community.

At the local creche, a bundle of kids waited to be picked up after play. A private enterprise only affordable to those who had work, resented by those who did not, reflecting the exclusion that comes with market supply in the absence of public responsibility or interest.

With water a familiar story: broken taps but which you can turn on with a spanner – if you had one, that is, or could borrow one. And if not, you rent one from a neighbour. The trouble with the supply was that it was random, not just interrupted. In other words you could not plan your day because you never knew when it would come, a constant stress, which for those who could afford it was easily sorted. You paid a tap attendant, one with a spanner, who would fill your bottles when there was water in the pipes. All of this a burden on those who have least and for whom, we have learnt, less is rarely more.

In the early evenings, people huddled around open fires for cooking and keeping warm, more 'black carbon' deposits into the atmosphere. And everywhere, clutter, not the clutter of possession that one normally associates with informal settlements, but rather the clutter of waste, of effort and things, waste of hope and opportunity, the clutter of people dumped as if they themselves are waste, everyone blaming everyone else for the way things are.

People's aspirations were best summed up by the following sign:

Joshua The Cobbler
These shoes are made for walking – AWAY

This was a horrible place to grow up in.

Lessons

For most in the development business and those who have seen the pathological conditions in refugee and other camps, all this is perhaps familiar. Odd somehow that familiarity should make it all the more ordinary, even acceptable, the way it is going to have to be for some! It was, however, an example of a community as if turning in on itself, waiting to self-destruct. Everyone on this third day of looking and listening reflected on how one might intervene in this most hopeless of places. How could the simplest of practical interventions be justified if it would play into the hands of the power elite? Could all the cartels' and groups' informal or illegal enterprises be mobilized rather than threatened in any attempt at upgrade? Or should everyone be moved, again, in which case where? What in any case induced the state of affairs in the first place – what are the primary causes of all the symptoms we had observed? And then there are even bigger questions:

- What would it take and how long to target more strategic inter-ventions – eviction, displacement, corruption, rights – or is this all someone else's business?
- Should we integrate, rather than isolate, existing power groups within community, however corrupt or marginal?

- How do we engage the kind of divided community we see when there is no sense of belonging, no commitment to stay or be involved?
- How should one deal with displacement and resettlement, both formally as with the example at the start of this chapter and informally as a result of evictions? Targeting the vulnerable, dealing with vulnerability, improving security?

3

PROFILING VULNERABILITY

After three days of looking and listening, we had a session on vulnerability and social exclusion – in particular in cities. We wanted to try to make more general sense of what we had seen and heard in Thawra, in preparation for our own planning and design exercise, back on our designated site.

We started with the usual stark reminder, from our conclusion in Chapter 1, that by 2030, 4 billion people will live in cities – 1.4 billion in slums. These 1.4 billion will, in different ways, be poor and on the front line of suffering the shocks and stresses of fear, insecurity, illness, uncertainty of work or of future. The UN's State of the World Report in 2007 estimated that '60 million people, roughly the population of the UK, are added to the planet's cities and suburbs each year, mostly in low-income urban settlements in developing countries. Unplanned urbanization is taking a huge toll on human health and the quality of the environment, contributing to social, ecological and economic instability in many countries ... Around a billion urban dwellers – a sixth of the planet's population – are homeless or live in crowded tenements, boarding houses or squatter settlements, often three or more to a room ... They are often exploited by landlords, politicians, police and government.'[1] All these people, one way or another, and despite their resilience to bounce back after crises, are vulnerable. Removing or reducing vulnerability and building resilience are central to the objectives of all development programmes and to sustaining livelihoods.

Vulnerability, however, particularly when targeting its root causes is problematic in various ways.

Drawing boundaries: first, how do we draw boundaries around a condition that is constantly changing where people go in and out of being vulnerable – and in a globalized world, where risk may be induced in one place and vulnerability experienced in another? Most risk, indeed, is experienced by those not responsible for its cause. Bangladesh, for example, with a population of some 150 million faces regular devastation due to rising sea levels and more cyclones induced by climate change, with all the associated risks to everyone. Yet in 2004, the average contribution of each Bangladeshi to CO_2 emissions was around an eighth of that of each US citizen.[2]

Type: the second problem is to do with type. There are, for example, vulnerabilities and risks associated with natural and man-made hazards, in particular in relation to the physical location of urban settlements – flood plains, steep inclines, at the edge of railway lines or in the wake of polluting factories. Increased densities, the rapid and largely unplanned growth of cities, the occupation of marginal or unstable land, the scale of informality, all contribute to degrading the environment. They contaminate water sources, reduce soil filtration capacities and increase the illegal or inappropriate dumping of hazardous waste. Mumbai's density for example, is around 34,000 persons per kilometre square, compared to London at 4500. Mumbai has grown by 1180 per cent since 1900, London by 10 per cent. Fifty-six per cent of Cairo's population live in informal settlements – one in three city dwellers in countries of the south live in slums. In Rio, 1.6 million people live on land classified as unsafe. In Sao Paulo, 75,000 people are periodically affected by floods and 25,000 are at high risk from landslides. In Manila, some 1.5 million or 31 per cent of the city's population are squatters on land subject to flood. In Bogotá, 1.3 million people live on steep slopes, subject to landslide.

There are, we know, two ways of reducing the risk of disaster (disaster = hazard x vulnerability): mitigation and adaptation. While mitigation is about reducing vulnerability (reducing greenhouse gasses, reducing environmental degradation), adaptation is about learning how to cope – changing habits and routines that are sometimes embedded in the cultural norms of place. Adaptation, in other words, is about becoming more resilient, more capable of bouncing back.

'While mitigation may be a national agenda driven by international agreements (Rio, Millennium Development Goals (MDGs) etc) adaptation is intensely local. It requires competent, capable local government with a commitment to working with all the low-income groups. This is not present in most urban centres and not easily achieved.'[3] Participation, adaptation and the capacity to be resilient are themes we will return to in subsequent chapters.

Social differentiations and hierarchies also induce vulnerability, by class, caste, gender and other inequalities, by income poverty and, importantly in cities, income inequity. 'Because people move in and out of poverty, the concept of vulnerability better captures processes of change than more static measures of poverty.'[4] It adds another set of criteria for measuring the experience of poverty '... defencelessness, insecurity, and exposure to risk, shocks and stress ... vulnerability and its opposite security stand out as a recurrent concerns of poor people which professional definitions of poverty overlook'.[5]

While income poverty is everywhere, income inequity is particularly urban in character. The clustering of poverty is more evident in cities as are the inequities of difference that this creates. These inequities are accentuated by spatial types (the slum, the public housing estates, the privatization of neighbourhoods with their gated streets and public squares) as well as their proximity to each other. Growing inequity says the UN, whether by race or by income, lead often to 'negative social, economic and political consequences that have a destabilising effect on society'. The UN goes on to report that South Africa, Namibia and Latin America are the most unequal in wealth; the accumulative effect has been a deep and lasting division between rich and poor.[6]

What we need is a better understanding of the dynamics of poverty, of income inequity and of vulnerability in cities. We need to understand the inter-generational transfer of inequity that is often rooted in caste, clan and in gendered cultural norms. We need a better understanding of the inter-generational transmission of poverty and the constraints this places on social and economic mobility. How do people get into poverty and how do they get out and stay out? Why do some get back in? How do we break the life cycle of poverty? If we take the cycle below as an example, where best to intervene and in this respect, how selective can we afford to be?

Vulnerability is also induced by politics and political rivalry, by conflict or authoritarianism often reflected in top-down planning that, as with social vulnerability, may result in displacement, repression, exclusion or other forms of discrimination. The transformation of values in urban life, the search for identity and belonging, the need often for multiple identities, the transformation of community and the loss of place-based identity, where your status is earned by association more than by location, undermines a commitment to place and makes engagement with community tricky. It undermines the social capital of community and therefore the resilience of neighbourhoods, because you don't know where you belong, whose values you share and, therefore, to whom you owe your allegiance. 'The freedom to determine our loyalties and prioritise between the different groups to all of which we may belong is a peculiarly important liberty which we have reason to recognize, value and defend' said Sen.[7]

Sense of belonging, we know, is a resource, what Robert Putnam calls capital.[8] That resource gets lost in the kind of estates we visited earlier, and for those displaced as they try to rediscover their sense of belonging, which in cities is more plural – more networked, more heterogeneous, less homogenous. Communities in cities, in other words, are rarely entities, which often we assume and search for.

This search for entity is a leftover from the old days of master planning. It ignores the continuance of shifting values and interests that are inter-generational and inter-cultural of some whose notion of community is not just social and organizational but spiritual as well. And when it gets difficult to pin down, as it always does, we – the development practitioners – turn it all into something we do understand and can work with: an organization, a centre, a neighbourhood unit, a formal collective that can be a partner in that triad relationship between the state, the market and civil society. We attach to it a cognitive wholeness and then give it a hierarchal arrangement of leaders and managements with delegated roles and responsibilities and shared ideals that guide its purpose, which is accountable, transparent and according to some normative international standard – democratic. We bureaucratize it in ways that are understandable according to northern logic and to all those serial thinkers who populate bureaucracy. We turn it into a thing that can be controlled. We give it responsibility but not too much authority. And then we invite it to participate in *our* decision making process.[9]

And when we try to homogenize that sense of belonging in the rush to complete our participatory exercise, we wind up excluding those who don't fit – the hawkers, street vendors, the homeless, the squatters. We criminalize rather than socialize the socially excluded, because often our identities are defined not by who we are, but by who we are not. Witness the barriers and claims on territory in the places we visited in Chapter 2.

People who threaten our certainty of expectation are usually excluded – an expression of 'homo sacer', an old Roman law describing people 'outside of society', void of values – waste. In the old days of public housing, if you didn't belong or didn't fit (family size, problem families, too old to cope, homeless) you were dumped into one of those 'sink estates', those monuments to the aspirations of planners that littered cities – separate, stigmatized, stereotyped, but easily managed.

And listen to families: 'A man living in a society without acceptance from his own society feels he is not regarded like a human being. He is always discriminated against by his own. No one cares and gives due regard to him except during election time. He is branded informal. His job is informal. His living place is informal. His way of talking is informal. In short, everything around him is informal except his vote in elections.'[10]

We have encountered in our site visit communities of place, of culture, of interest and practice and those of resistance. We have seen the conflict or potential conflict between groups. But how do we engage with each, with networks rather than entities?

In this respect, the cultivation of choice when it comes to identity is one principal responsibility for all development practitioners, a central theme in participatory work, because the ability to choose, to adapt according to one's values, beliefs and aspirations, builds resilience and reduces vulnerability. It is a defence against having our identity co-opted by systems, by planning ideals or single-vision thinking. It builds our resilience to exclusion and to violence.

Social, economic and political vulnerability and exclusion all too often find expression in violence and insecurity within and outside the household. The insecurity for women, of long hours of work, of returning home in the dark, of going to the toilet at night because the shroud of darkness is your only privacy; the exploitation of women and children working in the informal sector;[11] the fear of parents sending girls to school who maybe assaulted or abused on their way, or even in school[12] – all increase the daily stress on households and render the already vulnerable even more so.

Violence erodes the assets of the poor, undermines resilience and affects livelihood security. According to Moser, structural violence is not just physical but often embedded in the social structure of community and can include exploitation, exclusion, inequity, all of which weaken life chances.[13] Poverty and income inequity – particularly when they coincide with inequity between ethnicities or religions, the absence of horizons, the loss of identity and self-esteem – all contribute to creating a context for the exercise of violence. Some 10–15 per cent of the public budget of developing countries is spent on fighting crime. The World Bank estimates that 2 per cent can be wiped off GDP in dealing with the different forms that violence takes.

Power and powerlessness are fundamental to understanding the causal factors that underpin violence and are often reflected in territorial claims witnessed earlier. The redistribution of power, therefore, in urban programmes through planning, design and the democratization of governance is key to reducing violence – a long-term strategic objective of participation, partnership and good governance.

Finally, violence polarizes social groups into 'enclaves' with a profound impact on residential urban form. It generates fear and insecurity, or the perception of insecurity not just of crime but also a fear of 'other' – a fear of difference, as we had noted on our visits. What follows, as Charlotte Lemanski points out in her excellent studies of Cape Town,[14] is a withdrawal from public space into private enclaves, making public space – the streets and squares and parks – unsafe. It creates an architecture of fear. This retreat from public space promotes more inequity, more segregation under the guise of more safety. Examples of gatedness and withdrawal are everywhere.

When it comes to causes of vulnerability many, as we have seen, are already implicit in each vulnerability type. Environmental degradation, for example, or the unequal access to resources reflected in discrimination, or unequal power relations. When considering unequal impacts, how do we target intervention to the most vulnerable, without alienating others?

Violence, social exclusion, instability and insecurity we know are everywhere but most acute in cities because communities do not have the social capital or infrastructure, or traditional resources to solve their own problems. Cities offer less opportunity for community managed resources. The result is that it all places more dependency on the state and its professional advisors who often lack the will or capacity to respond effectively because, as we know, the state is poor because its people are poor – where the cost of collecting taxes is higher than their value.

In response, most governments and most aid, even the most worthy, will face the ubiquitous contradiction in development objectives between the moral obligation for equity or environment sustainability and the economic imperative to attract investment and enhance productivity. 'Achieving less ecologically damaging patterns of urban development will conflict with the priorities and profits of many powerful local and global interests.'[15] The result is the kind of aggression that passes under the guise of development, with its violation of rights, its vast displacement of people and environmentally damaging projects, all of which are fundamental causes of inducing rather than reducing vulnerability. Are these contradictions inevitable?

In 2003, Arif Hassan headed up a study of Asian cities undertaken by Asian Coalition for Housing Rights (ACHR) to look at the process of social, economic, physical and institutional changes and their impact on people, on government and on placemaking.[16] They took, for example, Beijing, Puna, Chang Mai, Phnom Penn and

Karachi. Their conclusions, reported in 2006, were discouraging. Poor communities were being evicted to make space for elite developments, driven by foreign investment. Due to relocation away from town centres and centres of work or schools, transport costs and travel times had increased. Incomes had been even more adversely affected because women can no longer find work close to home (94 per cent in India, for example, are self-employed, 60 per cent of household income in Bangladesh is generated by women). Informal settlements in and around cities had become denser to take up the extra population who had refused to move to resettlement sites in the peripheries. Conditions in these settlements had therefore deteriorated, despite all the efforts at slum upgrading.

Furthermore, in the drive to attract foreign investment, the nexus between politicians, bureaucrats and developers has strengthened and, therefore, zoning regulations and by-laws in cities have become easier to violate in the interests of capital, not people.

The report gives an example in Karachi, of a beachside park built to improve the waterfront and provide added amenities to people. To do it, to clean it all up, they evicted the hawkers, the small traders, seashell vendors and performers – the life of place – and replaced them with expensive food outlets and kiosks that the poor could not afford. A small charge was levied to use the park, legitimate maybe, but that effectively excluded the poorest. The result: a gated place that divides rather than integrates.

The park, like so many of city plans, like our site earlier, represents an ideal, imagined in the minds of architects or planners, where form-making takes precedent over social space, a confirmation of who belongs and who does not. It represents that single vision of what cities and city places should be. This kind of ideal, the single vision of quality and class are an expression of expulsion because you have to remove people, as if clutter, in order to do it and place them behind clear demarcations or enclaves. It's all about eviction and exclusion and mostly directed at the poor and most vulnerable, a worldwide phenomenon.

Presenting his master plan for 2021 for New Delhi, the India Minister for Urban Development was guided by three priorities: 'obliterating the slums (which house 60% of the city's 15 million people); taming traffic; developing a Manhattan-style skyline. All height restrictions on building will be lifted, except in a few historical places.'[17] In Daravi in Mumbai, home to 600,000 people with a thriving economy, clearance in the name of 'City beautiful' will displace families into high-rise concrete blocks, albeit with a promise of a toilet for all!

'Every year, millions of people around the world are forcibly evicted, leaving them homeless and subject to deeper poverty, discrimination and social exclusion. Often there are large-scale mass evictions where entire communities of tens or even hundreds of thousands of people are removed.'[18] So said the UN-Habitat Advisory Group on Forced Eviction. They went on to suggest that the reasons are many: tenure insecurity, development and infrastructure projects, large international events including the Olympics, urban 'beautification' initiatives, property market forces and gentrification, conflict, ethnic cleansing and more. Much of this is done in the name of development and part of the aggression that comes with development. Evictions in a selection of seven countries that the Advisory Group surveyed showed that 'over 10 million forced evictions were reported in just these seven countries between 1991–2005. 250,000 businesses and houses were demolished in Lagos – one of the worst offenders; 400,000 in Beijing in preparation for the 2008 Olympics; 700,000 residents and informal traders is Zimbabwe's "Operation Cleanout".'[19] In Cambodia, the government's sale of land to foreign investors – Russians, Ukrainians, Australians and British, mostly to develop the tourist industry – has displaced thousands of poor people into shanty towns and rooftop squatter settlements.[20]

The UN report points out that formal evictions are illegal and unjust. In 1993, the UN Commission on Human Rights declared that 'forced evictions are a gross violation of human rights' and run counter to Millennium Goal 7 that aims to achieve 'significant improvement in the lives of at least 100 million slum dwellers by 2010'.[21]

We wound up our evening with one of those never-ending discussions on the complicity of development practitioners – architects, planners and the rest in urban programmes, Olympic or resort villages, our co-option by market forces or powerful government officials, seduced by careers or money or a sense of wanting to achieve, an ambition to point to success and feature in glossies in the midst of all the mediocrity and failures.

In summary, an agenda of big issues for policy and practice emerged:

- contradictions in development objectives – bridging the social and economic imperatives of development;
- vulnerability, exclusion, insecurity, violence – integrating those agendas in the policy and practice of urban development
- understanding the dynamics of poverty, of income poverty and income inequity as an integral part of development planning;
- rethinking and unravelling the concept of community, the value of partnerships, and how we engage with it all;
- giving due consideration to the transformation of values, the search for identity, the question of loyalties;
- cultivating choice and widening opportunity.

PART II

PLACEMAKING AND THE ARCHITECTURE OF OPPORTUNITY

One has to be an artist to survive as a poor person –
you have to imagine space where there is none.

Resident of Rio Favela

REFLECTION: GETTING ANSWERS TO QUESTIONS YOU DON'T ASK

I was fresh out of college, armed with a professional degree in development planning. I had the state-of-the-art in planning tools – questionnaires, number crunching software and understanding of a dozen ways of representing data analysis. I landed up in the team implementing a prestigious project on Urban Risk Reduction in India, a first of its kind. It was an ideal place to deploy my skills.

One of the project sites was a slum in the bed of the river Yamuna in Delhi. There were hundreds of families living in congested hutments in the riverbed, on the wrong side of the embankments. Naturally, they were getting flooded during the rainy months every year. It was a highly vulnerable community at obvious risk.

We descended on the slum, with a well thought out and coded household questionnaire. After going through the initial round of gathering background data about the family, the questionnaire moved into gathering detailed information on the flood risk and coping systems, since that was the highest priority risk.

What came out of doing the first round of interviews was a complete shock. Floods were way down at third place on the list of threats perceived by the local residents. People said they knew how to live with floods, since they had been facing them for the past 25 years and also because the timing of the floods was very predictable. They had a local system of keeping a watch on the upstream waterworks and the level of water near the settlement and sounding alarms for quick evacuation as the levels rose. On the other hand, lack of schools for children emerged as a high ranking perceived risk factor. We tried hard to explain that they have not understood the term 'risk' properly and that absence of schools does not qualify. In response, an articulate young woman from the slum argued that if her son got good education then in a few years he would have a job and they would be able to move out of the slum into the nicer residential colony nearby. This was a far better risk-reduction option according to her than our suggestions of improving the drainage and building dykes while remaining in the vegetable vending business and continuing to live in the slum.

It was a truly eye-opening moment. I was completely stumped. This woman living in a slum had a long-term vision, while mine was myopic. She had answered a question we had never asked. We hadn't asked these questions simply because we had not even the vaguest of ideas about the existence of these very local and invisible issues when we started to design the surveys. We returned to our little office and spent hours discussing this predicament. Things had been turned on their heads. All our training seemed hopelessly misplaced. Someone thought of a prank and we sat on our computer and fed all the names of house-owners along with past experiences of disasters into an SPSS spreadsheet. We split the names into two categories – those up to five characters long and others longer than that. One click and our computer told us that persons with longer family names were more prone to disasters! That was the last time questionnaires and SPSS were used in our office.

That was my entry to PRA and community action planning (CAP). The tools were like children's games – and initially seemed embarrassing to indulge in as a professionally qualified urban planner. Yet they yielded amazingly useful information and did so in a really fast, easy and fun way.

The following years were a continuation of this education. We worked in the small town of Rohtak, near Delhi, where local groups came up with innovative ideas of terrain mapping. Rohtak experiences floods almost every rainy season. We organized a community workshop with local representatives, many of whom were teachers owing to the large number of educational institutions in Rohtak. During the brainstorming, people started putting the height of the high flood line, as experienced in recent floods, on a sketch map. Soon we had a bar graph showing the flood levels in different colonies of the town. Once inverted, it gave a topographic profile, which matched fairly accurately with the contour maps of the survey department! Local wisdom and innovative information gathering processes could yield accurate, inexpensive and instant information that was as good for our purpose as the expensive high-tech one. Our target audience could relate to this people's terrain map better than the technical contour maps and eventually the community workshops led to an action plan for maintenance of the drainage system so that floods could be minimized. Low-tech was not only faster and economical, but also found better acceptance within the community.

I now work as a consultant to communities, translating their knowledge and aspirations into plans and proposals and helping them to articulate and present these to governments, donors and their own selves for implementation. I also work with students and young practitioners to show them this other way of practicing architecture and planning. To show them that low-tech is good. To show them that people know best.

Anshu Sharma

By now, we were ready to contemplate again our own site, to explore design and planning interventions based in part on the lessons and reasoning we had witnessed locally, as well as the knowledge and examples we had gleaned globally and some, more theoretically.

Back on site, we would be looking for clues for where best to start to upgrade, where first to intervene and later how best to consolidate these beginnings into place specific interventions that would improve conditions and contribute to building resilience, reducing vulnerability and sustaining livelihoods. Unlike the usual data hungry and extensive survey of needs and aspirations – that search for a comprehensive understanding of everything before we start – we start instead, to find out. We would be looking and listening, measuring and mapping in order to gain insight into the conditions of life and the life of place. We were like urban acupuncturists looking for interventions that could release the energy latent in place and, with it, the capacity to self-improve or recover: small interventions to release strong and lasting ripples that would pervade extensively. We would be looking to get something started quickly and visibly, a catalyst or series of catalysts, with immediate, practical impact to generate interest and mobilize effort.

We were some 20 participants in this phase of the programme, made up of people from various factions within the community, as well as representatives from the Urban Development Authority, the Housing Authority, the Department of Arts and Education and our counterpart local NGO. Among us also were a number of young professionals – both local and international – there to contribute and learn. There were planners and architects, surveyors and engineers, and from the local academies anthropologists, epidemiologists and lawyers. Importantly and innovatively, the team included various artists keen to engage in urban regeneration.

It was, in principle, my task: a training programme designed to inform participants on the tools and method of Community Action Planning (CAP) and Strategic Action Planning (SAP) and in parallel, to jump-start the upgrading process. We were all housed in a makeshift building at the edge of an empty patch of land central to the settlement, earmarked by the authorities as a 'public open space' with no specific intent so far. Our makeshift building would one day become a fully equipped community centre for which the Council already had plans.

I sketched out a work plan and mapped out our agenda that we might follow over the next week. Nothing definitive, or set in stone, but clear in intent and arguably in bias. An agenda that would build policy or induce change from practice, to reason it all backwards. Our overall intent: to meet the needs of now, while working toward the aspirations of soon and later. It was to put together a Strategic Action Plan and then look for concrete ways of working towards it.

The work plan illustrated in Figure II.1 identifies various routines, with a variable sequence but all of which need to be covered: we need to map needs, aspirations and assets (see toolkits Chapter 4) and analyse then prioritize problems and opportunities. We need to be sure to identify not only symptoms of problems but secondary and primary causes as well.

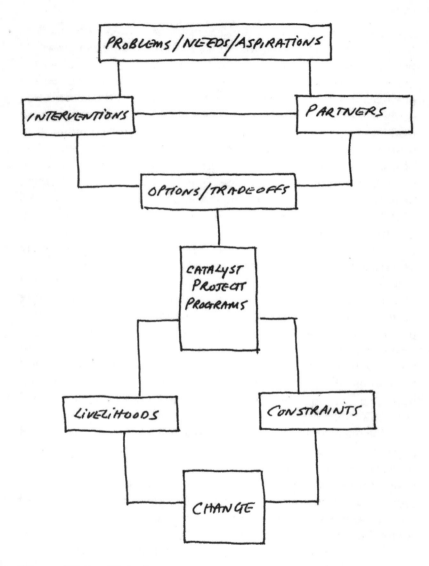

Figure II.1   *Work Plan*
Source: Nabeel Hamdi

We need to decide appropriate and immediate interventions – a range of options each of which we will initially analyse in terms of trade-offs: trade-offs of time, money, technology, political viability, capacity, for example. For housing, we might look at alternative delivery options, construction methods, technologies, tenure and management. For water, we might also review forms of delivery and management, as with other utilities.

In all cases, we begin to identify possible partners at the earliest stage – between community groups, between formal and informal private enterprise, between all and respective government departments. We will be doing our stakeholder analysis of risk and comparative advantages (see Figures 6.2 and 6.3, pages 95–96) while at the same time building a sense of trust and cooperation.

Early on, we will identify catalyst projects to get it all going, to meet needs and build confidence among all that something will happen.

Progressively, we will analyse the constraints to getting the catalyst going and equally to scaling it all up. What constraints are there likely to be for implementation? What or who will get in the way and why? Which constraints will be by necessity a context for our work (in other words, we have to accept in the short term) and which can be managed, removed or got around? We will need to deal with at least two sets of common constraints: the first is programmatic, to do with, for example, institutional capacity, political will, money, corruption, site conditions. The second is to do with discrimination relative to gender, ethnicity, status and more, many of which are often embedded in legal and regulatory frameworks.

Throughout, we will give definition to vulnerability induced by fear, insecurity and poverty and will consider livelihoods. We will map these vulnerabilities as well as the assets both tangible and intangible – skills, materials, land, belonging, neighbourliness and all the other social, physical, financial, natural and human resource assets that our interventions will help build.

And then we will need to give due consideration to all that will need to change in order to achieve results now and to scale up the impacts of it all (see Figure 11.1, page 171). What changes will be demanded (now, soon, later) in order to deal with problems and implement options? What changes in professional attitudes, work routines or habit? What to standards, what to legislation and power relations that open doors for people to access resources of knowledge, materials, land, money? What changes to method or organization of work, to partnerships and relationships between insiders and outsiders if we are to deliver on the strategic aspect of our planning? What does it all mean for policy?

Finally, we will need to add a number of specific considerations for scaling it all up quantitatively, where programmes get bigger in size and money; functionally through integration with other programmes and organizations both formal and informal; politically where programmes and communities can wield power and can become a part of the governance of cities; and organizationally where the capacity to be effective increases – when real change can be triggered.

And then, after we have been through the process illustrated in the work plan above, and as work proceeds, we turn the work plan upside down and work at it backwards, evaluating our progress: what had changed, how had livelihoods been cultivated and how had constraints been removed or managed? What range of additional catalyst projects were now needed in this second phase of moving things on, which we then evaluate in terms of trade-offs and partnerships? And how could one quantify the benefits of our interventions in so far as meeting the needs and aspirations we set out to fulfil? Had aspirations been compromised, given the circumstances ... and then we would work our way down again ...

4

TOOLKITS

My first session, after the usual formalities, was to bring everyone up to speed with the toolkits of action planning, planning for real, PRA and more.[1] We briefly reviewed some of the more commonly used bits of the menu, and some hints on how we might go about our initial tasks – things to prepare and watch out for.

Looking (direct observation) enables the planning team to see for themselves the conditions of the urban setting under consideration. It enables us to spot clues that will lead our enquiry, to check information on maps and plans that may already be out of date, if they exist at all. It will enable us to form a first opinion about how things work, based on a variety of observable indicators: inadequate water pressure, poor maintenance, fenced off gardens. Puddles will tell about poor drainage, accumulating garbage about the efficiency or appropriateness of solid waste collection. The planning team would observe the kind of small enterprises already in place, who plays where, whose turf is protected and how, what constitutes an edge or border and what boundaries have been fenced or walled, who shops where.

Transect walks are a useful way of organizing observation, offering a quick insight into differences in the settlement. Walking with local people, observing, listening, asking. We can organize our walks in mixed groups, or separately with children, women and the latest arrivals, elders – each of whom will offer a different opinion. We may also organize our first observation at three levels at least: the house, the settlement and more widely using rickshaws or other simple vehicles to observe relationships between this settlement and its neighbours. In their presentation, transects can be collaged or indeed performed as animation using puppets and narrative.

Figure 4.1   *Presenting transect information:*
BUDD student work at the DPU, UCL

Source: Supitcha Tovivich

Looking parallels closely semi-structured interviews: listening to
the needs, problems and aspirations of local people – shopkeepers,
women, children, elders, teachers, police and other key informants.
Stories and oral testimonies will tell how and why things work or
do not work, and who suffers and benefits. Why is one household
with water and their neighbour without? Who buys services
from whom, and what are the relative dependencies and power
relations implicit in individual perceptions of fear and vulnerability?
Individual interviews, community or group interviews, focus group
discussions, field diaries are all useful techniques.

While looking reveals information about the visible structure of
place, interviews tell about the hidden social and economic structure
of community and can be formal or informal. Formal interviews
are typically guided by questionnaires and by specific questions to
which interviewers need answers. Informal interviews are usually

conversational and conducted in familiar settings, involving open questions where one advances gradually, takes one's time and uses the vernacular in language and style.[2] Sensitive questions are carefully led up to and questions that can be answered with yes or no avoided: 'What do you think of the mayor?' instead of 'Do you like the mayor?' Value judgements implicit in questions are best avoided ('your back yard is full of rubbish!'). Failure to listen, helping the interviewee to give answers, asking vague questions (what do you think of empowerment?), engaging only with the articulate or those who speak your language are all to be avoided.

Looking and listening are usually supplemented by measuring and counting – a process more quantitative than qualitative but which offers additional precedents for the sizing up of roads, walkways, plots and for deciding acceptable distances to standpipes, the nearest clinic or school. We may count the number of service connections, establish where the highest land values might be and then look at where the greatest commercial activity occurs. We can attempt to correlate the relative percentages of public–private land to the likely burden this implies on local authorities for maintenance and administration. We might measure land utilization percentages, circulation lengths, area, ratios and densities – all indicators of the wealth and proper functioning of urban areas.

Then there are a bundle of techniques for harvesting the resources in community – all the capital or assets latent in place. We might do talent surveys to get a sense of the human capital resources we may have – who can do what, if there are teachers, carpenters, plumbers, builders, car mechanics and the rest. And then there are the physical resources: whether someone owns a truck or rickshaw that may be rented to transport materials, or if space exists in schools or houses for the new nursery or community centre, or if others own tools they may be prepared to rent or loan, whether empty land can be turned into community benefit for play, agriculture or new housing. Much of this resource harvesting can be done by community groups themselves, in part to tap their knowledge and information but also to get a sense of what they see as resources and what are not (the wisdom of elders, their capacity for dialogue, moonlight that improved security – which may not feature on our list of resources), partly also to sensitize people to resources that they may not recognize as useful but which are: their social networks or ability to improvise.

Much of this information can be diagrammed, mapped, modelled, or even performed – all useful means of documentation and communication avoiding, as needed sometimes, the bias toward literacy. At the early stages in the planning process, seasonal calendars, timelines, daily routines, pie charts, can tell much about the structure of community, the effect of seasonal climate variation on work habits and on the ability of people to cope. Many of these can be generated by community groups and need little graphic sophistication. Problem or conflict trees are useful, not only to get a sense of the impacts and symptoms of problems but also their root causes. This offers a chance to look at the practical needs of now, dealing with symptoms and also the longer-term strategic changes needed to tackle root causes, as illustrated below.

Diagrams are also a useful way of capturing the visions of people – sketches that may give emphasis to rebuilding family or authority.

Mapping and modelling are overused terms in today's participatory planning but are, nevertheless, useful participatory tools for documenting information and aspirations and of expressing views and opinions about place in a non-confrontational setting. The focus for all is the maps and models and not the individual offering the opinion, concern or idea. Cognitive or social maps, for example, map events in people's past and present experiences and can reveal social and political relationships that will need to be considered when preparing proposals. They can link the distribution of resources with caste, religion or other population patterns, to get a sense of who controls resources and therefore of power relations, which will be key in opening access to the most vulnerable when meeting basic needs and sustaining livelihoods.

Cognitive and social maps, on which everyone records perceptions, feelings, sentiments, prejudices, wants, needs and suggestions, are large in scale. Information is layered progressively using paper and glue and, equally progressively, themes begin to emerge with which to structure the planning process, about physical

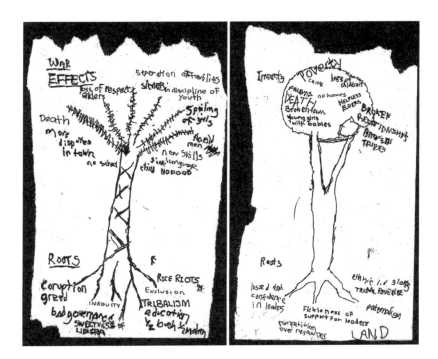

Figure 4.2 *Two conflict trees drawn by mixed groups of men and women, showing their perceptions of the root causes and impacts of war (Yealla Town, Liberia)*

Source: Sarah Routley: MA dissertation entitled *Peace and Peaceability*, a case study of Yealla Town, Liberia, 1998

problems, about fear and insecurity, about power relations and people with influence, who goes where and when, who uses what and so on.

Simple models of parts of the settlement made of scrap materials can detail issues specific to parts of the settlement, at a larger scale. Planning for real models, made in easily transportable pieces of rigid corrugated card, enable people to evaluate conditions in their own part of the settlement and then to place proposals for improvement that can be prioritized later according to now, soon and later. The collaborative process of making maps and models helps break down

Figure 4.3   *Forkpa and Isac's vision of peace in Yealla Town: Building Community (left); Building Family (right)*

Source: Sarah Routley (as for page 73)

barriers between 'them and us' and builds a sense of cooperation among participants at the earliest phase of planning.

Among all the other tools (brainstorming, prioritizing, group works and intermixing) games and role play are sometimes strategically employed in action planning to build awareness and sensitize professional or government officials or community leaders to key issues. Some games will be designed to simulate actions (if you do this, then this is likely to happen), others to teach skills or build awareness of planning procedures, potential hurdles in the planning process or familiarize people with planning jargon.

Sometimes, within the context of planning, role play can be used to build awareness of the needs and desires of groups of people who may not be well represented during the planning phases. Or indeed, to sensitize mixed groups of professionals who may be shifting from their conventional role of provider to that of enabler – how would

Figure 4.4   *Making models: BUDD student work at the DPU*
Source: Supitcha Tovivich

you play out an 'enabler' role in the planning of shelter or water or education?

Picture analysis is often a useful way, in gaming, of highlighting differences in perception and values of self, or others. People are asked to describe what they see in any one photograph or drawing and to discuss how conflicts may develop from different understanding of the same visual image, all of which will be valid. The purpose here is to build an appreciation that differences need not be threatening but can add to the richness and diversity of place.

Tools are the means with which to achieve ends. All will have limitations, and most times, in the swamp of practice, one finds one has to adapt or invent tools as one proceeds. Mapping, transect walks, role play and model making generate knowledge and socialize differences, which is an important prelude to engaging people as partners in the design, implementation and management of places and programmes.

5

KNOWLEDGE

We organized ourselves in various ways, using the toolkits described above, to begin to understand something of the problems and opportunities in our settlement. At first, we role play – each group designated an expert task – the housers, health workers, solid waste managers, enterprise and small business entrepreneurs, land rights and tenure, water, sanitation. The exercise is blandly called 'Getting Information'. Each group is asked in respect to its expertise – what information do you need? Why do you need it? How will you get it? How will you use it once you have got it? The exercise has four objectives.

First, given the mix of disciplines and vested interests in each group, each will have from the start a different take on, for example, the meaning of shelter or rights, the value of water and enterprise. What do we stand for and value in our definitions?

Second, it induces a debate on the values and bias each expert group will have in respect to its topic, and therefore how selective it will be with the information it needs in order to do its job effectively.

Third, we would discuss significant overlaps in information between groups, emphasizing therefore, the need for synergy and the pitfalls of looking within topic groups or disciplines. For example, housing will be as much about houses as it may be about rights, enterprise and improving health.

Finally, we make the point that what we the experts are after is the least amount of information to get going, rather than the most we can get. How best should we mobilize the information, knowledge, wisdom, aspirations of people, without the preponderance of study and analysis?

Out on site, we knew to avoid the linear process of conventional planning – survey first, then analyse, plan, and later, implement. We need to recognise that each phase of our work should make a tangible difference from the start, building progressively a sense of belonging and ownership in parallel with fixing things up and making it all work.

We used a variety of participatory techniques to become mutually informed. We used picture analysis to find out something of the fears and delights of people in and around the settlement – a quick and active way of getting it all going. Five snapshots, each of places outside that you like – places of joy and happiness – and five that you dislike or fear, for whatever reason; and likewise inside – your house, your school, your clinic. What we got in less than a day was a landscape of issues and places, both real and perceived, which we erected as a mural some 20 metres long at the edge of our work place.

There were pictures of people waiting in line – a hate of someone, to waste time waiting your turn at a health clinic – telling us much about discrimination (the poor had to wait in longer lines, the shorter one were for those who could pay), about capacities (not enough nurses); faces of hope or despair, places of memory and play – and other places of fear or resentment. There was the open fire out in the street – a like (warmth) and dislike because of the smoke and because it was your only warmth at night. There were pictures of latrines 'clogged with smell' and those of locks on lavatory doors, preventing access – someone who was charging a small fee for use.

Over the days and weeks to come, people gathered to talk, to add comments or photos, or graffiti, embellishing it all with notes and blobby paint and scratches and Post-its. Nothing was protected and some pictures were obliterated or even removed. It began the process of dialogue of how people felt about their place, which we would occasionally formalize with focus group discussions – what did it all mean for women and children?

Later, we turned the mural into a mosaic or music (songs or rap) or poem – a way of socializing groups of children and youth, building organizations with whom we might engage later as

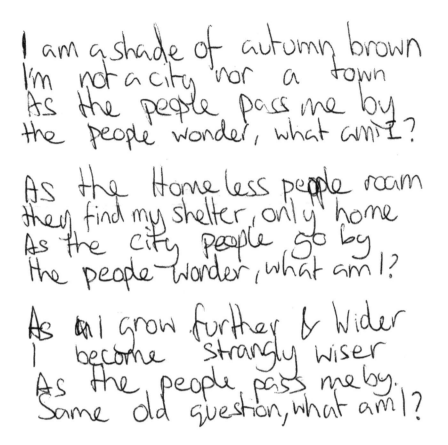

I am a shade of autumn brown
I'm not a city nor a town
As the people pass me by,
the people wonder, what am I?

As the Homeless people roam
they find my shelter, only home
As the city people go by
the people wonder, what am I?

As I grow further & Wider
I become strangly wiser
As the people pass me by.
Same old question, what am I?

Figure 5.1 *Poem*

Source: Pupil, Acland Burghley School, London, 2005

partner on physical planning. At the same time, tapping into the emotional experience of people and having fun, which is a key to engagement.

We borrowed from United Nations International Children's Emergency Fund (UNICEF) a format for capturing aspirations – another layer of understanding to help shape our planning. We started with a phrase 'If I could I would...' to be completed by anyone in words or pictures or song or poem. Some we completed through random encounters; other times, we were more selective, differentiating aspirations based on gender or generation. Aspirations were usually very modest. 'If I could I would have windows in my house' (they lived in a container with only painted windows to make it look like a real house). 'If I could I would watch more TV'; 'If I could I would have a door to my bathroom'; 'If I could I would make my house fly' – a love for home but a need to escape from here and now.

Our harvesting of needs, emotive attachments and aspirations was coupled with the harvesting of tangible resources – skills, talents, enterprises, innovations, materials and equipment. It was an asset mapping exercise of physical and human resources, and in particular of social capital – networks and alliances and neighbourliness not easily visible – the kind that reflects the resilience of community to the shocks and stresses induced by the loss of employment, fear of eviction, or illness including the growing threat of HIV/AIDS. 'For many people in informal settlements, social networks provide an extremely important resource and for the many individuals and households affected by HIV/AIDS, community support can be extremely valuable. For example, people are able to rely on their neighbours to assist with food, care and shelter ... Neighbours can often assist in caring for younger or older members of the household ... The disruption of these social networks and support systems can result in greater isolation.'[1] This we had already witnessed in the bleak landscapes of the project we had visited earlier.

In our subsequent maps, we wanted to begin to localize problems and opportunities and even ideas of what we could do to deal with problems, rather than wait until the 'analysis' was done.

We made a map of the whole or bits of the whole at 1:200 scale using the techniques of 'Planning for Real'. Large sheets of corrugated card – the kind one uses for packing cases – with an outline of the settlement drawn on to them. Some rough three dimensional buildings were cut from construction paper, scored, folded and pasted on. On these maps, using bits of paper and with the help of our graphically talented architects and planners, we wrote or drew cars, or rubbish, or trees and placed these on the maps.

Figure 5.2   *Area mapping and (below) detail mapping: ideas for a community facility*

Source: Jeni Burnell (top) and Nabeel Hamdi (bottom)

There were comments and suggestions, some of which would be contested. The rule was you could layer the maps with your own views and in contradiction of others but you could not remove any bits. Where a particular part of the model became too dense with information, or where we needed more detail, then we would scale it up to 1:50 maybe and continue the process. These maps were also laid outside our meeting shed, but easily carried in and stacked at night or when it rained. They would fill some 30 square metres of floor area – an installation in their own right laid out beside the mural. They were fun to make, interactive and yet not intimidating, colourful, dynamic. People would discover from murals and maps something about themselves and each other and about the place in which they lived.

In a separate exercise, children had made a map of their own school and experience of life in the settlement. It was drawn on a loose linen bed sheet with indelible magic markers and patched with scraps of old material that they had sewed on to indicate trees, houses, cars and the rest. They would carry their tapestry to where the mural stood, pin it up on the wall and explain it to anyone.

As ideas proliferated (people had always known what needed to be done and how to put it right but had not had the means or legitimacy) so we would build a 'thought fountain' in the same public space we had occupied with murals and maps – something visible and again transformative – getting people's opinions of what they might do to put things right, right from the start, and make things safer or cleaner or happier. It was designed by two of our local artists and was made up of a series of dangling wires, strapped to a wooden pole with a metal collar, each wire with a bulldog clip at its end. Some were short for children, others taller.

People would write or draw their suggestions, or add photos of houses or playgrounds as precedents and clip them to the fountain. And when there was no more space on the first fountain, we added another with everybody's help, and another until there was a forest of fountains filling the place, telling its story of place and making space for ideas. With it all came a sense of ownership of what would become a place of information and learning, as much as a place of aspiration and memory.

Figure 5.3 *Information gathering and the transformation of place: mural*
Source: Nabeel Hamdi

Figure 5.4 *Information gathering and the transformation of place: thought fountains*
Source: Jeni Burnell

On timetabled occasions there would be a storyteller – someone from the community and usually an elder – who would provide a narrative of the history of the place. It was aimed at children principally, as a part of their newly founded class in citizenship, but usually parents or passers-by listened in an open classroom. They would tell of the conflict that had displaced them from the north, their arrival here, what it was like when they arrived, the rejection they felt at first, how they had won their rights and built their first homes. Everyone would discover and respect all the different histories that made up their differences. This bringing together of differences, in stories, in maps, in picture analysis and learning would serve to build a spirit of cooperation, a vehicle for converging the interests of different groups, in order to build partnerships in the prelude to planning and doing.

The idea of the storyteller (and the place that was emerging on our site) I had first seen in Cape Town's District 6 Museum. District 6 was settled by black South Africans and evacuated during the days of apartheid, ostensibly to make way for commercial development, although today it remains largely vacant. A museum has been established in memory and celebration of the struggle for rights and the people who struggled against eviction. It is now a community centre for visitors, tourists and locals as well. There was a large map of the place imprinted on linen that occupied the ground floor, which you could walk on or sit on. Everywhere there are histories or people and places one can see and touch, rooms, as they were where you could walk into. And, most days, there would be a storyteller or event, recounting their experiences. Many of the children listening would recognize their names in the stories, of their grandparents or uncles or other relatives. They would become a part of the story and build a much stronger association with where they lived and with each other.

In our own place and in response to the demand to get something going quickly and visibly, which would run in parallel to the overall physical upgrading process, we started with something tangible and recognizable as a need. Our settlement was regularly flooded in the rainy season and snake bites were common. How could snake bites be avoided? What did you do if you are bitten? Where did you go and who could help? We had decided to do in it ways that were appropriate and fun – no flip-charts or Post-its, no Power Points or bullet points, but theatre instead. Street theatre, played out by professional actors paid for with money from the Department of Education and the Council for the Arts. It was directed at children – 15 minute events using puppets and music. Later, we looked at ways of mitigating the floods themselves.

In time, what started as an unused and derelict piece of land adjoining our shed became a place of theatre, history, information, learning – an exhibition or urban 'interpretation centre' for insiders and outsiders, even for tourists as a part of their 'homestay'. This invitation to others served to break down barriers between them and us and to integrate more this settlement into the social fabric of the city at large, to make it a destination. What was implied was an unlikely partnership between the National Heritage Museum, the Tourist Board, the Urban Development Authority and the Department of Housing and, in its various ways, the slum community.

For now, however, there was a pause as we begin to sift through the information and to consider the kind of themes, problems, opportunities and aspirations that might help to shape our next interventions. How would we now move? There had been nervousness among some of our group about our presence as outsiders and the role that we were playing. How much were we disturbing it all? How does one decide when you have done enough or when and where to intervene more robustly in the interests of equity or efficiency, or what to leave alone? How does one recognize when 'intervening becomes interfering?' What roles and responsibilities had one assumed and in whose interests were these being exercised? These issues we will return to in Chapter 8, in our discussion on PEAS.

For now, there had also been much discussion among our group about the tools and techniques of participation and also a need, it seemed, to reflect more thoroughly on some practical theories that underpinned it all – to get up to date with some of the latest thinking on the strengths and pitfalls of participation, before moving on. What is participation? Where and when do we need it? How do we know that we know enough about place and people to start with planning and doing? Who and what might get in the way and how do we manage the inevitable conflicts of interest or opinion or priority that are bound to emerge, or the primacy of one set of ideas and demands and authorities versus any other? How do we reconcile the debate in favour of processes that rely on local knowledge and local action, with those that are transformative of power relations and national institutions?

6

PARTICIPATION IN PRACTICE

We started our session with a short and simple role play. Its purpose was to give definition to the term participation from the points of view of some of the principal actors in development, in order to reveal some of the conflicting agendas and also the complementarities. Moderating the dominance of one actor's agenda versus another, converging interests and negotiating priorities is one of the key roles of facilitation. The exercise served as an introduction to the practice of participation and sensitized participants to issues of power relations and differences in practice. It was also a useful vehicle for training facilitators in negotiation and conflict mediation techniques. In any case, it got everyone thinking, before I started talking.

We formed into mixed groups and designated a role to each group – an international NGO, a donor, the local authorities, municipal engineers, a community-based organization, and a local constituency of the political party in office. I asked each group to consider in respect to participation why they thought they needed it and when. Later, we would consider what each group might need to know before they start. What might get in the way of doing it and why? These questions were, of course, the participants' own questions derived from the first weeks of work and discovery on site and their own perception of the term and of themselves, which I now asked them to consider in groups.

After an hour or so of group discussion, I asked each to present their reflections in general before we got into more detail. What was participation and why did we need it? The responses were predictable and served to illustrate the range of definitions in current use, in relation to differences in purpose. Each group had conformed to stereotype, to their own silo of self-interest and occupation.

The NGOs were driven by ideals – by the '…exercise of popular agency in relation to Development'.[1] Participation to this group was about community building, about sustaining livelihoods and tackling the symptoms and, where possible, the root causes of poverty. Their concerns were with rights, the right to citizenship and all the other rights enshrined in the UN Convention on Human Rights. They talked of reducing vulnerability, building community resilience and giving community voice. Their concern was with building capacity so that civil society could engage effectively in governance and markets. Participation, they said, was the life blood of all socially intelligent development, mobilized locally and transformative, institutionally and politically.

After the routine applause to a worthy summary (no one dared disagree!), a local man sitting next to me turned and muttered, 'Their dreams are punishing because they are not reasonable and not reachable – not here at least.' It was as if he felt threatened more than enlightened.

Markets – market enablement and market liberalization – drove the donors. Participation for this group was about giving space to encourage informal and formal enterprises wherever possible. Governments acted as enablers rather than principal providers of goods and services, preferring instead to 'stimulate growth and competition' to facilitate access to land, credit, services and building materials for small scale (community-based) enterprises, formal and informal.[2]

They talked of 'stakeholder' participation and not just 'community'. Participation, they said, improved the recovery of costs. It helped policymakers reach decisions that were equitable and efficient and widened choice. This in turn fed markets and stimulated growth.

Our group of politicians was keen to extend and consolidate their ability to govern – to help the poor but at least public cost and without alienating their political constituencies, mostly among the middle classes. For them, participation was central to the democratic reforms of public institutions – whether in education, health or housing. It was good for votes and for attracting aid. It was good for devolving responsibility but without devolving too much power. 'We want to involve people, but without losing control', someone said. I wondered to which rung of Arnstein's ladder they had ventured to climb![3]

For the local authority – their municipal engineers and others – participation was about improving efficiency in the operation and maintenance of services and utilities and the delivery of shelter. It was about partnerships, which took the load off municipalities and, again, contributed to improving governance. Their take on participation was aligned to definitions of partnerships – pragmatic and business like. 'An association between two or more persons, groups or organizations who join together to achieve a common goal that neither one alone can accomplish ... Each member agrees to contribute resources with the understanding that the possession or enjoyment of the benefits will be shared by all. Partners work hard to strengthen each other and to endure conflict and change, because they recognize that their shared goal extends beyond the reach of any one member.'[4]

None of this invokes the language of rights or the social imperatives of empowerment, nor is it intended to do so. However, implicit in their text is the mutual recognition of ownership, the pooling of resources, the building of resilience to endure conflict and change, the sharing of aspirations, or at least of some objectives.

Our community group took on an activist's stance, situated somewhere between the debate on tyranny and transformation. Their position is best summarized in Figure 6.1 (overleaf).

To them, participation was ideological in purpose, political in substance, pragmatic in its outputs. The concept of partnership depoliticizes participation, they said, and was no more or less than a neoliberal plot to get governments and their cohorts off the hook. Participatory processes had at once to meet the needs of community now, as well as the broader and more strategic objectives of 'social justice and radical political change' in order to guarantee citizenship, reduce poverty and tackle exclusion. 'Extending the concept of participation to one of citizenship also recasts participation as a right, not simply an invitation offered to the beneficiaries of development.'[5]

Figure 6.1 *Poster produced during the Paris student demonstrations c.1968*

Source: Arnstein, S.R. (1969) 'A Ladder Of Citizen Participation', *Journal of the American Institute of Planners*, Vol. 35, No. 4, p. 217

Meanwhile, most times and whatever the debate, communities do participate in programmes, often initiated by outsiders, not because they agree with their high ideals or even the programme that these outsiders bring, but because if they do get involved they might just get something, which, after all, is better than nothing!

By the time it was my turn to talk, most of the ground had already been covered. With the help of an ageing overhead projector and a few of my usual plastic overhead transparencies, I tried to summarize and fill in some of the gaps.

I started with an assumption that wherever you were, whatever you did and however you did it in development work, participation is central to all planning of programmes and projects. I then reflected on a snapshot of history reminding everyone that the early reformers, Geddes and Howard, neither of whom happened to be planners (Geddes was a marine biologist, Howard a stenographer) placed people and the 'Social City' at the heart of their ideals for planning.

Geddes, for example was vitally concerned 'that the ordinary citizen should have a vision and comprehension of the possibilities of his own city'.[6] He said that 'for fulfilment there must be a re-absorption of government into the body of the community. How? By cultivating the habit of direct action instead of waiting on representative agencies.'

And then there was Howard with his vision of the social city and his insistence that the new cities of tomorrow should be the common property of the inhabitants and that the increase in land values should belong to them and not to property speculators, to be used for their common and cooperative purpose.

Ownership, direct action, governance and community, the common good – high ideals indeed, ideals it seemed we had returned to in our discussions on participation, in search of meaning and value in design and planning.

I went on with a definition I like, neither tyrannical nor seemingly transformative, not at first. Participation is about taking responsibility with authority and in partnership with other stakeholders in pursuit of common goals. And it is everything else that everyone else had said already. Responsibility, because with participation come rights and also obligations. Authority, because without a large measure of control and self-determination, you cannot have ownership and without ownership you undermine commitment, over the longer term at least. And partnership, because it demands cooperation, not just to deliver on needs but also to forge alliances vertically with other authorities and horizontally with your own, which in time can influence politics or policy and which can both empower and transform.

But we should be aware that '...empowerment and transformation require not just the opening up of participatory spaces to debate transparently citizenship ... but also the more prosaic transformation of everyday life: relief from the burden of queuing for and carrying water, of hand tilling fields, of dependence on relations, of patronage for daily subsistence, of the burden of care imposed by diseases ... Transforming the notion of participation into one of a radicalised and political citizenship ... doesn't suddenly do away with the costs of participation ... In the short term, the disadvantages (to the poor) of confronting unequal relations on which they depend, may simply outweigh the costs of acquiescence.'[7]

I recalled the plea made by Rose Mulokoane of the South African Federation of the Urban Poor (FEDUP), addressing the UN-Habitat Governing Council in 2007: 'Don't call us beneficiaries', she said. 'Don't call us end-users. We want to be your partners. What we want you to do is to include our inputs in your policy... If you don't include our ideas in your policies, it will be just a beautiful policy, like a beautiful lady without a husband to marry.'

We now know that the process of participatory work depends on what you are trying to do and what you can achieve relative to where you are. Its history and development as an ideal is already reviewed in Hickey and Mohan's excellent book *Participation*, as have its transformative values in power relations and policies through the mobilization of 'popular agency'. But what of the practical values of participation: why do we need it?

We have already seen that working across the usual interests of communities and other stakeholders is a good way of defining needs – that combination of desire and necessity. It's a good way of converging vested interests rather than contesting their legitimacy, and of getting accurate information. That is, information made useful through a cyclical process of interpretation offered by different interest groups.

It is often said that there is no greater evil in project planning than a problem misstated or stated in a way that is incomplete. It leads one in search of solutions that wind up tackling symptoms rather than root causes, to 'Band Aid' interventions that may be necessary in the short term – practical but not very strategic. The interpretation or triangulation of information is important in this respect.

In one example, there was a demand from community to improve the lighting in their settlements and so reduce accidents. Our first response was more street lights. But the accidents people referred to were largely associated with violence, as it turned out, rather than vehicular or work related. And it was mostly in our discussions with women, children and ethnic minorities that this emerged. Targeting the vulnerable, understanding exclusion and mitigating fear were all primary causes of insecurity and demanded a bundle of responses, more long term, more strategic. Street lights, on their own, are Band Aid interventions, necessary but incomplete in response to the problems as later discovered and defined.

Participatory programmes, in the early stages of planning, also help identify areas of potential conflict among groups vying for power or competing for resources. They help tap the ingenuity of people to discover ways of solving problems that may not be a part of the expert repertoire. They enable '...the construction of alternative versions of the world, to fashion networks of solidarity, and build people's confidence in their own knowledge and capabilities and with it a sense of entitlement'.[8]

Participatory work reduces dependencies on state or other organizations and can create the opportunity for new kinds of organizations to emerge, providing continuity, once the outsiders pull out. The Women's Bank, and all other informal enterprises worldwide, are good examples.

The question throughout, however, is who initiates these programmes and why? Who really benefits? What are some of the conditions that ensure success?

Unquestionably, one of the key conditions to effective participation is strong local organization. Building that capacity among local groups to become effective partners is both a reason for, and an outcome of, participatory work. At the same time, engaging with already established organizations may be playing into the hands of the very people whose hold on authority one is trying to disturb, in order to encourage inclusion of others who may be excluded. Political goodwill, ownership of problems not just solutions, finding a common cause and engineering common goals, building trust, ensuring good representation – not just in presence but also in voice – are all conditions to cultivate so that efforts can be sustained over the long term. Importantly, participatory work must produce tangible results progressively, as we have seen in our earlier work, so that trust and confidence can be maintained. But what do we need to know, or at least beware of, before we start?

In all these respects, we do need to know something of the type and structure of community and of existing organizations and hierarchies. How do we engage with communities that are networked, as they mostly are in cities, rather than place based? How much can you engage with people and organizations who are either transient or see themselves as transient, and whose aspirations and sense of home are, therefore, elsewhere, even if they have been in place for 20 or 30 years? Who is included and who is excluded? Is it by choice, necessity or coercion? None of this will become obvious, although it may be evident before you start, which is why starting is a good way of finding out. Flexibility, group work and intermixing, stakeholder analysis of key actors and conflict analysis are all useful tools in this respect. My preferred tools and routines are diagrammed below.

Whether in workshop format or otherwise, I asked a variety of groups – at first based on gender, age, ethnicity, and later perhaps by trade or occupation, and later still based on location in their settlement – each to consider who were the primary, secondary or external stakeholders and what each group thought would be their interests, influence (authority) and priority with respect to upgrading, housing or infrastructure improvement. And then, who might we partner with – who can help, when and how? I

Stakeholders Analysis			
	Interests	Influence impact of interest on the Project Positive (+) or Negative (−)	Relative Priorities of Interest
Primary Stakeholders			
Secondary Stakeholders			
'External' Stakeholders			

Stakeholder: Persons, groups or institutions with interests in a project. Primary stakeholders are those ultimately affected, either positively or negatively. Secondary stakeholders are the intermediaries in the aid delivery process.

Interests: Relate each stakeholder to the problems which the project is endeavouring to address.

Influence impact: The extent to which stakeholders are able to persuade or coerce others into making decisions, and following certain courses of action.

Importance: The priority to be given to satisfying stakeholders' needs and interests through the project.

Figure 6.2   *A sample framework for doing stakeholder analysis*

Source: unknown

might do the same with analysing potential conflict. What were the compatibilities in behaviour and goals between key actors – government, non-government private sector and donors and all the factions which make up communities?

ANALYSING CONFLICT: THE SQUARE

A possible working definition of conflict is: a *relationship between two or more parties who have, or who think they have, incompatible goals.*

In order to understand more deeply what conflict is, it can help to focus on two elements in this definition: behaviour (which is basic to any relationship) and goals (what you want to achieve). The model below identifies different kinds of conflict according to these two elements. The word "compatible" means "in harmony with"; the word "incompatible" means "clashing", or "in opposition to".

COMPATIBILITY OF GOALS AND BEHAVIOUR

		GOALS	
		COMPATIBLE GOALS	**INCOMPATIBLE GOALS**
B E H A V I O U R	**COMPATIBLE BEHAVIOUR**	NO CONFLICT	LATENT CONFLICT
	INCOMPATIBLE BEHAVIOUR	SURFACE CONFLICT	OPEN CONFLICT

Figure 6.3   *Analysing conflict*
Source: Responding to Conflict (RTC)

What were the incompatibilities? Who could work with whom and who might get in the way of progress? What would need to change in behaviour or goals? Later, what would be the comparative advantages and risks of any partnership between actors, and where were there likely to be conflicts? How might these conflicts be managed?

Knowing the actors is an important prelude to participatory work. Knowing the advantages and risks they bring to project work helps build cooperation and breakdown stereotypes. Finding the common ground, sharing risks and mutual benefits, understanding both monetary and non-monetary contributions, sharing authority, responsibility and being accountable – all distinguish and define partnerships and are key to the practical implementation of participatory work.[9]

Finally, one needs to be sensitive to the culture of decision making in any one context – the respect for hierarchy or authority often embedded in social practices, the time and steps it takes to reach a decision. Some years ago, while working in Egypt on urban upgrading, I had arranged a meeting with a director of the General Office of Physical Planning (GOPP) who was responsible for urban programmes. I had scheduled a meeting at 9am and expected to be out by 10am. My schedule of issues for discussion was clear and precise: a review of progress to date, approval of the process we had set up and some guidance on how best to proceed. His office was large, with one of those heavy oak desks at one end, flags and trophies symbolically arranged – little or no paper or signs of work; on one side, a leather sofa with two men in discussion and on the other side, a meeting table with three others in dialogue.

I sat, we talked, tea was served. He would occasionally drop in on either of the other two meetings going on in parallel. Our discussion ranging from topic to topic was kept specifically unspecific – the politics of international aid, now that Egypt had secured the Camp David Agreement, his curiosity with my own background in Iraq, but with little or no Arabic, and the four years I had spent in Cairo as a child living in Zamaleck. He would offer his views on the complexity of urban planning in Cairo, from traffic to housing, the dangers of the informality of construction and the illegal subdivision and sale of agricultural land, which was continuing to sprawl, and his aspirations for the future.

Others in the room would eavesdrop or interrupt, offer an opinion or add a piece of information or insight. On occasion, the director would shout across the room for confirmation of fact or in support of an opinion. Then more tea. We did talk through my agenda but not in the structured way I had planned. His guidance on next steps was unspecific and uncommitted, as if from Confucius: 'Use your best judgement at all times', he said!

Establishing his status, winning my respect, sizing me up and getting the opinion of colleagues dropping in and out – all took precedent over specifics. We both knew that we each had other agendas that we did not discuss. But we established a good working relationship based on mutual respect and mistrust. Decisions would come later, tempered by the value of rewards, which might come our way: mine with careers, his to win office as mayor.

For our last session on participation, we formed back into groups and brainstormed some of the objections and constraints to participatory work, still common in practice, from all sides.

Most were predictable and were by now well known – and yet remained systemic to practice. Participation is professionally threatening and brings few rewards to architects or engineers. It interrupts expert routines. People get in the way of creative work, they clutter up the process. Consensus building waters down creative work to the lowest common denominator. It all takes time, raises expectations that can never be met and lacks efficiency. Some, the government officials in the group, said that participation can be politically threatening because it polarizes political constituencies and can make space for extremists. It often serves to reinforce existing leadership structures; gives dominance to the majority or elite and either way can exclude minorities. It winds up being oppressive to minorities and undermines their sense of belonging. In any case, it all demands a high level of agency coordination and the kind of long-term capacity that government does not have.

Some argued that participation could often override established and sometimes indigenous organizational structures in the interest of equity, the kind decided by 'them' from outside. It undermines traditional methods of making decisions based usually on trust, on friendship and kinship, which outsiders will label as nepotism or corrupt. Rather than polarizing it normalizes radical engagement.[10] Importantly, it co-opts knowledge and the voice of the poor in promoting outsiders' agendas, in getting answers that agencies want to hear. It empowers outsiders.

'One of the most substantial appropriations of data in international development has been the World Bank's Voices of the Poor project. Word processing at its most literal, the uttering of poor people around the world has been collected, translated, selected and discarded, edited, collated, categorized, copyrighted and given an ISBN ... That these commodified voices can now be purchased in three volumes, written in English, for a total of $60, suggests that poor people have no psychological or literal ownership of something claimed to be theirs.'[11]

Finally, there was the cynical view, of those looking to save money and safeguard the interests of management. To them, participation takes too long and costs too much to do, and in the end its benefits were difficult to measure. And if you can't measure it, it can't be worth having. How do you quantify it all in money or other indicators, especially in the short term that the project cycle often demands? It was Oscar Wilde who said a cynic was 'someone who knows the price of everything and the value of nothing'.

Diana Warburton, in her paper for INVOLVE on 'The True Costs of Participation', and in search of its real value, suggests the concept of 'public value' focusing on outcomes, services and trust beyond the usual 'efficiencies' criteria. The emphasis here is less on 'how much' you spent but more on 'how well' public resources are spent – and what was achieved. 'How can you put value on democracy?', she asks. 'Of course democracy and participation will always have moral and philosophical value attached to them which cannot be subject to such measurement. Yet INVOLVE's reviews found research showing that Swiss Cantons with more democratic rights than others had, on average, about 15 per cent higher levels of economic performance. Robert Putnam's famous research in Italy showed how social capital affected democratic activities and economic performance and Nobel Economics Laureate Amartya Sen shows the correlation between democracy and eradicating famine...

But with the development over recent years (by the Community Development Foundation, the New Economics Foundation, and others) of ways of measuring complex benefits of participation such as trust, neighbourliness, community involvement and community vibrancy, there is beginning to be a greater understanding of the practical benefits that participation can offer – to local and national governments, participants, communities and the wider society – in the short term and over time.'[12]

Before we got started back on site, I had asked participants to reflect on examples of effective participatory work, ones that started with need and then scaled up in power and influence for communities, a practical intervention with long-term strategic value. Pooja's example in Pune, India, embodied all the characteristics that we hoped to achieve during our own project work – an excellent example of the power of participation when carefully cultivated. She had researched the example as a part of her work for me at the Development Planning Unit (DPU), for a course I run on Participatory Processes: Building for Development.[13]

'In cities in India, sanitation facilities are provided and maintained by local agencies affiliated with the government. This includes building toilet blocks in poor settlements. But perhaps due to the growing population in cities, the need is far greater than what is planned for, even though resources allocated for sanitation often remain under-utilized.'[14] When toilets are provided, traditional ways are used in cost evaluation, hiring contractors and generating tenders. The engineering department carries out the process without consulting community members. 'The agencies responsible for construction and maintenance generally have little accountability to the communities in which they build, and there is no sense of ownership among the inhabitants or their organizations for the new toilet blocks.'[15]. Frequently, the quality of the toilet block structure is bad; water supply is minimal with poor drainage. Toilets are maintained by workers hired by the municipal agencies and are not accountable directly to community members. Consequently toilets are usually left dirty and community members have to pay an additional price for the workers to perform their duty and clean them. Important maintenance and repair work is ignored and toilets become unusable leading to people using open spaces close to the toilets for defecation. Such unsanitary conditions cause serious health problems leading to high infant and child mortality rates. Women are especially vulnerable because in order 'to protect their modesty, they often wait until nightfall to defecate in the open – but this need to wait until dark also causes widespread gastric disorders'.[16]

'Solutions such as "pay and use" toilets charging 1 rupee per use, proved to be an extremely expensive alternate for poor families to use every day. In the 1980s, the Alliance (SPARC [Society for the Promotion of Area Resource Centre], NSDF [National Slum Dwellers Federation] and Mahila Milan) received aid from international donors and proceeded to do community-managed slum surveys to demonstrate the need and inadequacy of public provision'.[17] It built toilet blocks to demonstrate the capacity of community-based organizations. In 2001, the Alliance won a contract for building and maintaining community toilets in the city of Pune, where it had been 'supporting a vibrant saving and credit movement among women slum dwellers'.[18]

Involving the community in the design and building of the toilet block helped empower locals and build community capacity. The Mahila Milan initiated savings groups, and members pooled their money into savings accounts. These savings were then available to be used in forms of 'crisis loans' and help finance infrastructure projects like the community toilets. With the help of the Alliance, community groups also did surveys and mapping exercises to understand their needs and present themselves comprehensively to city officials. 'The Alliance also builds their skills in mapping services, settlements, resources, problems, etc., so that they get a visual representation of how their present physical situation relates to them. These maps are also particularly useful in developing plans for improvements with external agencies.'[19] Although many were illiterate, some women learned about building materials and techniques in order to be able to oversee the construction process. 'In the beginning, we did not know what a drawing or a plinth was. We did not understand what a foundation was or how to do the plastering. But as we went along, we learnt more and more and now we can build toilets with our eyes closed.'[20]

'As more women's groups understood how to manage and oversee construction, they reported more confidence in interacting and negotiating with government officials during weekly meetings.'[21] 'Learning new skills such as mixing cement and other construction work will allow individuals to be better supervisors as well as increase their chances of getting better jobs. By allowing community members to supervise and make decisions in the project, important characteristics of leadership and entrepreneurship are developed. Community members learn to handle negotiations with local authorities in a positive community-building project instead of over issues such as evictions.'[22] Additionally, 'The people who build them [community toilets] take their experiences to other settlements, other cities, and become trainers themselves. In this way, the evolution and refinement of ideas occur in practice, in different situations.'[23] This process of learning and teaching within slum communities facilitates knowledge, creates a wider information base and enables more communities to self-engage in community development projects affecting them.

'With community input, each toilet block built by the Alliance is different depending on community requirements and specifications. However, common improvements include more ventilation, better quality buildings with different entrances for men and women and also take into account safety handles for children and the disabled. Some toilet blocks include a community room where people can convene and socialise. Community toilets also included a room for the caretaker to live, ensuring his livelihood and housing, thereby allowing community members to negotiate lower wages. Ultimately, the cost of the toilet blocks was 5 per cent lower than projected by the local authorities. A monthly pass for 20 Rupees per family using the community toilets was introduced significantly reducing budget costs for toilet usage in households.'[24]

With the help of the Alliance, community members were able to be more than mere 'recipients' of services and their intensity of participation met all four levels. In the initial phase, community members designed the toilets and the Alliance built 114 toilet blocks. The municipal authority provided the 'capital cost of construction', electricity and water supply. The Alliance and community organizations 'designed, built and maintained the toilet blocks'.[25] As community involvement increased good governance characteristics like transparency and accountability increased as well. Weekly meetings were held to discuss progress and issues, maintaining communication with all stakeholders, the government officials, NGOs and community members. During these meetings, community members were central decision makers and able to decide on costs and location. This was demonstrated by local women's groups who negotiated with traders to reduce costs for raw materials being used in construction. Also, with the support of the Alliance, the now 'experienced' community members were able to share their knowledge and experience working as partners with local authorities, with members of other slum settlements.[26]

'The Alliance was awarded more contracts by the city government and was also invited to Mumbai by the Municipal Corporation to initiate a bigger programme in partnership with the World Bank to build 340 toilet blocks.'[27]

7

INTERVENTIONS:
SITE PLANS AND HOUSE PLANS,
BUFFALOES AND MUSHROOMS

We had reached that stage of the programme when we were ready for planning. As our agenda for the day, we set out some of the recurring themes that had been identified from our surveys and mapping of needs and aspirations and started a discussion with everyone about next steps. We started with aspirations before we searched for catalysts to get it all going. One of the recurring aspirations, but without much specification, was the desire to make it all a 'good neighbourhood'. In our discussions of what this might mean, we had the usual wish lists, a summary of ideals from some of the maps: improved facilities, usable open space, accessible streets, a market place, affordable and improved standards for housing, more trees, playgrounds, clean water, toilets for all, more jobs and the rest. Then someone said 'A good neighbourhood is a wonderful place to grow up in.'[1] This statement was about quality of life and well-being. This would be determined partly by the wish lists offered by others, partly also by the spatial and physical arrangement of places and significantly by the way in which place would make space for social development, for building community and a sense of neighbourhood belonging.

Deconstructing this simple and yet provocative aspiration invoked many of the strategic aims, dangling from our Thought Fountains – the primary causes of so many of the problems we had encountered. They set a number of goals to aim for in project work. Safety, and fear of eviction, from the occasional violence against ethnic minorities from petty and yet sometimes violent crime and getting to school safely; ownership and belonging, expressing the desire to call it all your own, to be in control of one's own life, to decide on what is best for family and community, rather than have it decided for you, if at all; opportunity for work and play, being connected city-wide rather than isolated, to resources, schools and markets – to other communities; health and well-being was another theme, including healthy eating, awareness of disease and its causes and how to safeguard against disease and stay healthy – washing hands, good nutrition.

As we layered these initial aspirations derived from inside with others, by others from outside – improving and sustaining liveli- hoods, promoting good governance, ensuring rights, cultivating choice – a very different and more strategic set of agendas and professional responsibilities emerged. It all seemed to demand a very different kind of planning from the usual physical and spatial master plan if these agendas were to be integrated into the regeneration of place, and a very different kind of professional that our trainees and students would reflect on later. What do these themes mean for housing, for water and sanitation, for social space, community centres, for getting to school, and all the other practical interventions common and necessary to regeneration?

We started the next phase of planning by looking at the next stage of catalyst intervention in parallel with our knowledge park – to meet needs and work toward our bigger goals. Our aim was to meet needs and aspirations locally but in ways that would trickle up to offer benefits to the plethora of other settlements city- wide. It would become a city plan made up of small, networked interventions, reflecting the multiplicity of visions and aspirations on the ground, rather than some single ideal imposed from above, or worse, from outside.

BUFFALOES AND MUSHROOMS[2]

Looking and listening, we came across one family – a man and wife and his teenage children – on the front deck of their self-built house. We got into discussion about their aspirations for a community centre in this settlement, which would serve everyone's needs, a place they could use for work and play, for meeting and performance, for enterprise. It was an aspiration voiced by many, often in different ways – a focus to their settlement, a place for young children to be cared for and informed, outside of school. Not a shed that they currently had but an icon, a piece of architecture to give them pride and status, like other parts of town. As we sat on their deck, enjoying their generosity (pineapples, coconut juice, curd, dates) with our pens and notebooks, I observed listening in the not too distant backdrop a buffalo – an odd sight in an urban setting – a small, quite stunted beast with bloodshot eyes and drooping ears.

It was a welcome distraction to our incessant questions, a point of casual discussion at first. Whose was it and what was it doing here? Sino, the father and Tiba the mother, turned out to be very conversant on the subject of buffaloes. It was theirs and they had called it Betty, after the kind woman 'from far away' who had donated it and five others to other families – one for each grouping of six families. Betty (the woman) was working for an international NGO and had explained 'the buffalo project' as a vehicle for rebuilding livelihoods that they were promoting as a part of their resettlement of people here after displacement from their coastal village. She and her colleagues were searching for ways also to rebuild community in the early days of resettlement. There were no buses, after all, so no bus stops to get the process going, which they had done so successfully in Nela's place on the other side of the big city.[3] And they had already learnt their lesson in community building: in the place, which we had visited earlier, that big community centre that had been built at great expense. The NGO had not been able to figure out how to dispense with lots of money, quickly and visibly and Betty (the buffalo) and her like were not as photogenic as a building, not least to all those sponsors wanting results. The centre, we will recall, stood empty because no one knew how to use it or manage it, nor indeed who owned it.

Sino and Tiba had nodded their way through endless monologues from Betty (the woman) on livelihoods, sustainability, self-realization, cooperation and trust building, which the buffalo project was to inspire. They nodded more out of politeness than understanding. She was, after all, well intentioned and had come a long way. In any case, they had accepted the gift of the buffalo, as had others.

Betty (the buffalo) spent her days grazing wherever, feet in some dank swamp or other, oblivious to issues of cause and effect, of livelihoods or sustainability. She was cared for by Sino and Tiba and their group of five or six families, the maximum she could feed with milk curd, and had become a family friend. Buffaloes, we were told (and there are many varieties) were a better source of milk than dairy cows as their milk contains twice the quantity of butter fat and is a source of cheese as well. They live longer than domestic cattle and deliver some 3000 litres of milk per lactation, over a period of about 300 days. Young buffalo achieve a daily weight gain of 800 grams without supplementary feeding. Buffalo cows remain productive until the age of about 20 years and can begin to calve at three years old. Buffalo butter fat is also a major source of cooking oil. They live on coarse vegetation and are an important source of protein. Their dung is made into patties, sun-dried and burnt to smoulder in the early evenings to ward off mosquitoes and is used as fuel for cooking.

The small group of six families who cared for Betty were a start in community building. They would cooperate in care and breeding and in reaping the benefits, although this had been difficult given the disparate nature of groups who had arrived here from different places and for different reasons. Many mistrusted each other. And when Betty gave birth, the group would keep the calf and pass Betty on to another group of six families with advice. Soon enough, the first group of 30 families would double to 60 and so on. They had all recognized, pretty quickly and without consultants, the advantage of pooling resources and 'federating' the grouping for mutual gain but, again, there were difficulties. They had neither the help nor place to set up their enterprise. And, like the Women's Bank, they wanted to avoid a hierarchal organization with its tendency to control and instead maintain the network of small five to six family clusters as their basic unit of organization. But they had not heard of the Women's Bank, neither had they had help. The buffaloes were gifted, with big ideals and then Betty (the woman) had left as quickly as she had arrived. In any case, soon there would be too many buffaloes. They needed to think of alternatives.

We had stumbled upon the beginnings of a narrative that would serve to discipline the design of their community facility. Later that day, we extended and enriched this narrative with other community groups, building on the aspirations of people and all their resources of talent and skill and speculating on outcome.

What they needed was a place in which to grow a community-based enterprise around the resources that buffaloes offered and scale them up to benefit everyone. There would be a place for some six or seven buffaloes to roam and graze and drink. A management team would be set up, consisting of an elected representative from each of the family clusters. The team would serve the interests of its own cooperative and then look to diversify and increase output of products and even calves for sale. They would emerge and become a higher level of organization.

There would need to be a place for making ceramic pots to pack the curd – a pottery, which might itself extend to making pots for other markets. There would be a place to weave and embroider cotton patches that are typically used as covers to curd pots. Much of this activity would be home-based. The centre would offer opportunities to socialize around work and for training. Someone had the idea of turning buffalo dung into smaller 'mosquito coil' type pellets, easily scented with herbs and then marketed as organic mosquito repellent, crude but effective. Then there would be cheese-making, their own brand of mozzarella, their own label. There would be training in book keeping and in marketing, offered through the Women's Bank, and later on a shop and cafe. This would be the start to a number of urban farms or enterprise centres nationwide. One could dream, in time, of a federation, a networked organization joining the Fair Trade Alliance and competing for markets.

Could we help, someone asked. Maybe we could, I thought. In my discussions with the Eden Project in Cornwall and with others in London, Birmingham and Torquay, we have begun to think of ways in which enterprise and other community-based organizations in urban agriculture and recycling can share knowledge and experience and more, how the filter of learning from south to north can be unblocked.

Not everyone of course was into buffaloes. Our harvest maps had also revealed an abundance of food growing in pots and cans, in rubber tyres and upturned car bumpers and plastic crates, on rooftops and in front yards. We were looking for ways of transforming dead space and turning it to productive use. Working with the artists in the group, food fountains were designed, installations were made of the same elements people were using in their homes and planted with a variety of vegetables and berries and colourful plants. Each installation, more vertical than horizontal because of the tightness of space, and its planting, would be an event, an idea first developed by the Slow Food Movement to transform public open space. It would be educational, profitable and fun. It would mobilize collectively the ingenuity of everywhere around using food to build more community, planting vegetables and ideas for reuse as well.

Other urban food initiatives were already underway, some emerging, others well established as enterprises, which we now visited. We were looking for ways to integrate these groups into new enterprise partnerships, but taking care not to undermine their autonomy. We needed to look at how much resource or organization they needed to extend, recognizing that too much would interfere and might disrupt their flexibility.

There were, for example, the urban mushroom farmers, a grouping of some 40 families, well established, growing mushrooms in the darkness of cupboards and stairwells, both for their own consumption and for sale. They had called themselves The Women's Development Society and had been helped with money and skills by a local NGO. Their mushroom growing generates a small community fund – invested in the cleaning of their local temple and in other local community activities. They had started as a voluntary organization and had emerged as a social enterprise. What they needed was a place for children after school and a meeting room. And if they could have a yard in which to make the organic brick from which mushrooms are cultivated, then they could double their output to households. A centre would also offer opportunities to engage with others and consolidate their marketing through well-signed outlets and markets, while maintaining the mushroom growing as a home-based activity.

Both they and the buffalo groups would invest in the maintenance of the centre through their common fund, the beginning, it seemed, of self-financing in part the centre, of owning it and being in control.

Then there were others – the furniture exchange – individuals recycling used furniture who might train others, and themselves emerge collectively as an enterprise. I recalled the writing of Nathan Straus, Administrator of the US Housing Authority in the 1940s in his 1945 book *The Seven Myths of Housing*.[4] In it and reflecting the tone of the times (instructive, a little patronizing) he describes the 'frontline rehabilitation clinic', a workshop with such tools as the management saw fit to make available, where tenants could repair their own furniture. A teacher, either employed by the project management team or made available by the local school system or by a local private welfare agency (NGO), guided tenants in their work. With the aid of a piece of material or a little paint, tenants were enabled to give new life and attractiveness to furniture. 'Incidentally', he said, 'a spirit of neighbourliness grows in a workshop of this character.'

Or indeed building on the idea of the Katrina Furniture Project where victims of the disaster that devastated New Orleans and its surroundings in August 2005, using in part material from destroyed houses and with the help of university students, staff and NGOs, made furniture and set up their own workshop managed by the community.

One could imagine adding a workshop for recycling or reusing waste into household products and building components, and through the enterprise centre, opening up the equivalent of Homebase or Home Depot (do-it-yourself stores) – the first possibly in a chain of community run enterprises, city-wide. It was all going on anyway, but with organization and more connections, it could all be scaled up in size and impact. If we could partner up the organizations with the formal equivalent of Homebase in country, then we could integrate these community enterprises into the larger national, even global, economy as key players. We had thought that

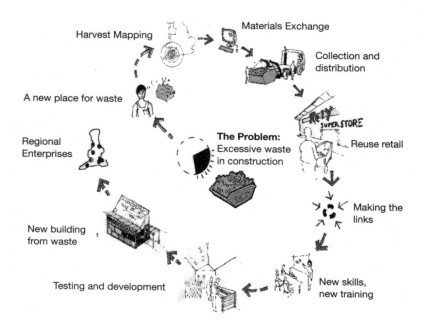

Figure 7.1   *Schematic, the building plot at the Eden Project*
Source: ASF-UK

the building of the centre itself could largely be made of local and recycled materials – a piece of architecture – an example of what could be done. It would itself serve as a training ground in building techniques and new crafts, a new urban vernacular that would grow and adapt as needs demanded. It could be financed in part by corporate sponsorship under the auspices of their corporate social responsibilities, in partnership with the community, the NGO who was mediating and local government.

It would all be like a laboratory, locally owned and managed and, in time, self-financing. It was all about partnerships, enterprise and livelihoods and importantly about building community and all kinds of assets.

THE PIEDIBUS

Other groups were working in similar ways, looking for interventions that would solve problems and generate ideas. One issue that featured recurrently during our mapping and discussions with families was how to get the kids to school safely, in the absence of a school bus. Equally important was how to give children a role to play, in planning. Even had there been a school bus, it would be difficult to access the narrow streets and alleys. We brainstormed ideas and settled on one that we had borrowed from Lecco in Italy – the Piedibus. The local authority would hire school bus drivers. Except they would not be driving buses, but instead guiding groups of children, eight to ten in each group, on foot to school. Some groups would meet at designated meeting points; others would collect children from houses. There would be eight groups to start with and more if needed. It would take about 40 minutes to walk to school for most of the children.

Occasionally the Piedibus would take a different route to school, through parts of the neighbourhood unfamiliar to children or thought to be risky or of special interest by parents. In this way children would get to know different parts of their neighbourhood, breaking down perceived borders between communities, stopping occasionally to observe and talk. It would be like a daily transect walk with children observing, recording, learning, informing. Later each of the groups would emerge as informal local area planning teams, each would appoint one member to sit on the Piedibus planning committee and brainstorm area improvements from their point of view. Two members of their planning committee would occasionally join the community development council and help decide improvements.

It would reduce greenhouse gases given the absence of vehicles, contribute to the health of children, improve security, give children voice in deciding improvements to their area and help build community. It was a practical intervention with lots of potential for strategic planning.

THE MOBILE MARKET AND RESOURCE CART

Then there was an idea for a mobile market unit that would enable local people to access nearby markets, simple to move, easy to make and adaptable to a variety of functions. It was in part a response to recent government initiatives, on site and city-wide, to 'tidy up' informal markets that were interfering with traffic and, in our case, an exposure to tourists visiting historic monuments on the other side of the canal. The idea was to regulate rather relocate, with some legitimacy, a market stall that could be combined into flexible linear or cluster configurations to suit very different locations. In addition, an idea that came up during our early discussions with men who typically wheel their barrows or carry their baskets to market stalls was for a mobile unit that could be wheeled or dragged by bicycle and in which they could occasionally sleep the night.

William's idea (a student of architecture at the DPU) was for a simple timber framed structure that could be clad with a variety of reused or recycled materials – timber boards, plywood, corrugated sheets, flattened soda cans, even cloth – tapping all the ideas and innovations that were everywhere throughout the settlement. Cladding panels would be designed to be foldable, to fold down as counters and up as sunshades in a multiplicity of ways. On top, the panels would unfold in concertina style and provide a skylight and headroom for sleeping.

Single units could be clustered together to provide larger units. The whole could be configured in a variety of ways and would occupy public space without the need for tenure or even legal licence.

We had thought that the units would be made at the Enterprise Centre's recycling workshops and could be sold or rented in flat packs to stallholders or retailers city-wide. Some would be bought by the municipality for regulating markets in other parts of the city, or as information booths giving advice on health or directing tourists, while supporting local community-based enterprises like ours. It might all start with a loan from the Women's Bank to the newly formed committee of largely male stallholders.

Each mobile unit or combination could serve as exhibits or installations in public squares and art galleries, demonstrating to everyone the art and inventiveness of people who self-build from waste, raising awareness among the general public, opening doors politically and gaining support for all kinds of social and environmental agendas. Some of the units in clusters of three or four could serve as small mobile tool shops or design centres, giving advice and information and hands-on training on what you could do with waste or recycled materials and how to fix up or extend your house.

It would all start with Betty the buffalo, her sisters and their mate Bill, with mushrooms and with those inspired enough to know that Betty and mushrooms served both a practical need for produce and money and offered longer term bigger in scale strategic opportunities. The logic of the process from which the centre emerged was implicit in the behaviour and actions of the everyday; the objectives of what to do now and what we could do next were derived in action. Like a collage, each step was pieced together in small increments; each move led to subsequent moves guided politically, socially, economically and artistically but without any precise knowledge of where it might lead. 'The urgent need is to design strategies and institutions that can better integrate incomplete knowledge with experimental action into programmes of adaptive management and social learning.'[5] We will return to the underlying rationale in more detail in Part III.

For now, we could see that what was emerging was less a community centre and more a place of enterprise and social learning. It was a hive of industry and innovation in capacity and building techniques, an urban farm and workshops with training activities and childcare, shops, a cafe, a laboratory of ideas and innovations, not just in product and design but in process and partnerships as well, in good governance and neighbourliness. All of this was in stark contrast to the community centre, austere and empty, which we had visited earlier.

Later, back at the knowledge park we thought, 'what if'? What if the urban farm and Enterprise Centre teamed up more formally with the national university whose campus was not far away? Their

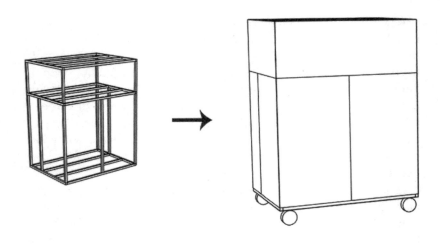

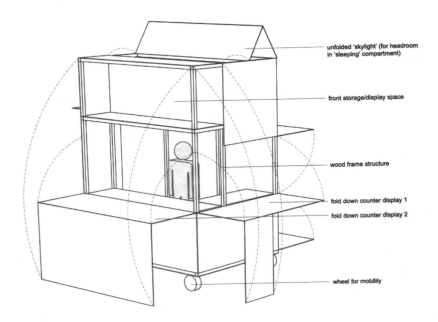

unfolded 'skylight' (for headroom in 'sleeping' compartment)

front storage/display space

wood frame structure

fold down counter display 1

fold down counter display 2

wheel for mobility

Figure 7.2   *Mobile market and resource centre*
Source: William Hunter, BUDD, DPU, 2008

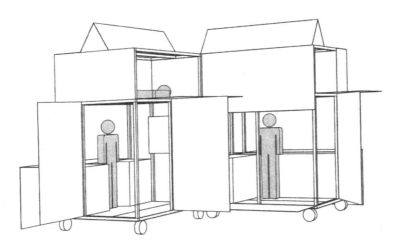

students were already involved, as were others internationally as a part of our team and training activities. It would all offer a field laboratory for students of social development, of planning and architecture and engineers, industrial designers and artists – all of whom are integral, potentially, to urban regeneration. They would offer their expertise and, at the same time, learn from the expertise of everyone and the everyday. What if some courses could be validated for academic credit? What if some of the international workshops and fieldwork, which universities in Europe and USA undertake annually, were to home-base here in community and exchange a Memoranda of Understanding with this community and their enterprise centre? We had already witnessed the growth in the status and connectedness of our centre to urban and possibly national systems (farming, trade, manufacturing) and reflected in titles – from Community Centre to Community Workshop, to Enterprise Centre to – who knows? 'The Thawra Enterprise Institute' with partners worldwide.

In ways like these, like others, we had started a process in which global agendas of governance and livelihoods would be localized and made place specific. At the same time, we had made space and created opportunity for local programmes to globalize, to feed the body of knowledge of design, planning and urban regeneration.

Our knowledge park, which we had established during the early phases of looking, listening, mapping and modelling, had cultivated learning, understanding and a sense of cooperation. The Enterprise Institute would cultivate partnerships and good governance around food and products in support of all kinds of livelihood opportunities. Both centres would attract tourists and all kinds of visitors (as they already had done on market day), as well as professionals and academics, the curious or adventurous. This sparked another line of enquiry...

HOUSING

Housing need and housing conditions had been key themes during our looking, listening and mapping, with the usual range of issues

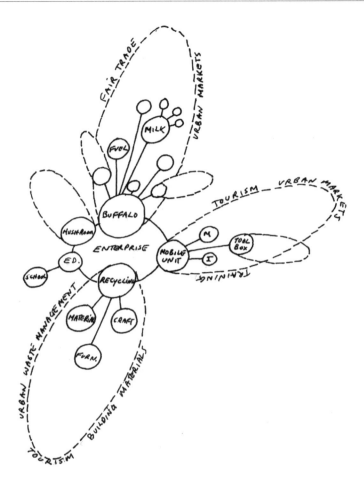

Figure 7.3 *Building community: partnerships, enterprise and social learning*

Source: Nabeel Hamdi

that needed to be resolved. Individual concerns recorded on maps included: overcrowding, lack of space for work or adequate sleeping space for children and extended family members, poor construction and inadequate sanitation. Fires were common in view of the density of the layout, the construction materials from which houses were built and the open fires for cooking. No one adhered to any standards of health and safety, not even those set by the community – not because they did not want to but because it would mean standards of construction and materials that no one could afford. And worse to many, the undignified appearance: it all looked like a slum, despite the few traditional houses still standing and visited by tourists. And still, after 30 years, there was a sense of insecurity of tenure; not so much from mass eviction but among the many individuals who rent from renters, and others living along the canal in full view of tourists and the historic monuments that are regularly visited, on the other side.

Before we searched for options and catalysts to get the improvement process going, we stopped to review the broader context into which this search must fit. What lessons have we learnt, internationally, what examples are there of good practice? What are the primary causes of some of symptoms we had observed? Importantly, we reviewed some of the key components that we will need to consider in our search for ways forward, which include: an inclusive and participatory process that consolidates improvement incrementally; land rights; security of tenure; appropriate forms of finance.

The figure opposite illustrates and contrasts the conventional planning process for housing – instant, prescriptive, in public ownership, with one that is mostly available to the poor.

We know from experience worldwide that when a progressive or incremental process is denied to the poor, the burden of investment all at once, and the repayment of loans, often pushes people back to the insecurity and vulnerability from which they came. Consequently, a comprehensive and instant plan to upgrade, with one-off capital investments or subsidies, to standards that are inappropriate functionally and financially, is unlikely to work. Processes like these profit investors and empower professionals and displace the very people for whom they were intended.

We also know that insecurity of tenure compounds poverty and is one of the most pervasive stresses suffered by the poor or vulnerable. Without tenure security, the poor are denied housing rights '...they are denied the right to organize, make claims on public resources,

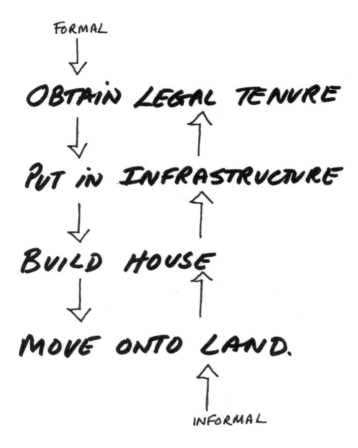

Figure 7.4   *The way things happen*
Source: Adapted from Ruth McCleod

or to participate in decision making processes that impact them directly ... The absence of rights is directly associated with the absence of investment by people living and working in slums. The population gets by but their productive potential is stifled and they are not able to contribute to the economic growth and socio-political vitality of the city, other than to offer their labour at de-humanizing wage rates, thus perpetuating their poverty further.'[6] On the other hand, formalizing tenure has also sometimes to be progressive and participatory moving, for example, from block tenure to groups of people to safeguard against individual evictions by landowners, while starting the process of registration of titles and eventually to more formal individual or even cooperative titles. Formalizing tenure, we have learnt, must be linked to improving income and building to affordable standards. If not, and particularly when on inner city land, poor families will sell out and return to unsafe or insecure land, preferring income to house or land, especially if they are tied into unaffordable repayments on loans. 'Properties in slum and neighbourhood upgrading programmes may be particularly prone to sale if, due to location, the plots are worth a considerable amount.'[7]

The linked debate on land and land markets is extensive and not for us to debate here, in any detail. It is worth remembering, however, in the context of our work that there will be in general two opposing positions in respect to the role that land plays in housing. Mark Napier outlines these to be on the one hand those who support the 'rights to land' and on the other, those in favour of the 'market enablement' or neoliberal position.[8]

The 'rights camp' argues the need for land security in order to build livelihoods and reduce vulnerabilities. Security of title, market protection from land speculation and a strong role for the state in land management and provision are all key to securing rights. There is a bias toward more land to be placed in state ownership in order to protect the interests of the poorest and to provide a safety net from speculation. And there is a case for a more active state role in the direct construction of social housing.

The 'enabling markets' view is that land is principally a financial and productive asset that, in contrast to the 'rights' camp, suggests that land use should encourage economic growth, creating employment opportunities for the poor. Safety nets, in their view, are best provided by, for example, income support or other subsidies and not by state held land banks, or land subsidies. Any appropriation of land by the state for social use should be at market value.

The 'rights camp' will critique the 'market enablers' in so far as they ignore implications of landlessness on the stresses of poverty and, therefore, on economic growth and social productivity. 'Land subsidies are one of the most effective means of leveraging the resource base of the poor, encouraging significant household investment in housing development and providing a base for the development of sustainable livelihoods.'[9] The enablers counter this view, because it restricts economic growth that is engineered, often through land markets (which land subsidies undermine), limits choice of location and is patronizing.[10] Reality, of course, lies somewhere in between and is constantly renegotiated given national political differences, international agreements (on trade, the MDGs) and the pull of international incentives to comply, coupled often to aid.

And then there is finance, another key and extensive component of housing. Our task here, in this broad-brush overview, is *awareness* of issues on the basis of which the expertise we may need can be identified. As Bertrand Renard has said, 'Cities are built the way they are financed'[11] and presumably financed in the interests of public or social values, as much as for market values. The relationship between finance, land and housing markets is intrinsic to successful policy.[12]

But in order to finance upgrading, the kind that places human development as a driving priority, and to tackle the root causes of poor housing, we need to search for models of finance where development and the poverty agenda are central to the objectives of physical improvement. We need to move beyond conventional systems of credit, of mortgage finance or micro finance that target individuals, to models of collective lending. We need to recognize the 'social power of credit'[13] that conventional economic theory denied, and with it the potential for social and not just economic productivity.

One such collective model we have already illustrated in Chapter 2 is the Women's Bank – an affiliation of a new global network of Urban Poor Funds. There are a growing number of other examples: SEWA, the Women's Bank in India; in Cambodia (Urban Poor Development Fund); the Kenyan People's Federation and the South African Federation of the Urban Poor (FEDUP). Diana Mitlin offers a succinct summary of its objectives:[14]

In ten nations, a new kind of finance agency, Urban Poor Funds, is working with federations of saving groups formed by slum or shack dwellers or homeless people. These funds support the members of these federations to obtain better quality shelter with basic services, by providing finance systems that serve their needs (including supporting their savings). In doing so, they also help to change low-income households' relations with government agencies and the law, as these households obtain housing solutions that are legal and that can be served by publicly provided infrastructure and services. This is achieved either through a move to new sites or through upgrading and legalizing their existing homes.

Mitlin goes on to explain that Urban Poor Funds are unusual in various ways. They are unusual in who they serve: those who are not otherwise eligible for loans elsewhere; in who owns them, with members – people, NGOs, professionals – all drawn locally; in what and who they fund – notably funding collectives as well as individuals, for the improvement of infrastructure or groups of houses; in building grass roots savings groups collective capacity – to manage investment, negotiate disputes, manage land, in support of a 'broader vision of societal transformation'. In addition, Urban Poor Funds help link actions and policy change, in that they set precedents for governments of solutions that work, which are collaborative rather than in competition with other government initiatives. Mitlin goes on to suggest that these funds use loans in ways that keep down debt burden and enable, as we have seen, groups to work at a local level and, at the same time, build city-wide, national and international movements. They recognize, in other words, the importance of scaling up to have impact and scaling down to have relevance – simultaneously and progressively.

For the next phase of work and back in the swamp of the everyday we now searched for alternatives for improving houses and housing conditions. Again, we wanted to respond to the symptoms of stress, with practical interventions, while working toward the bigger agenda of primary issues illustrated so far.

At first, we needed to organize, to break down the site plan into manageable organizational units with whom we could engage in planning, design and management, so that anyone who wanted to

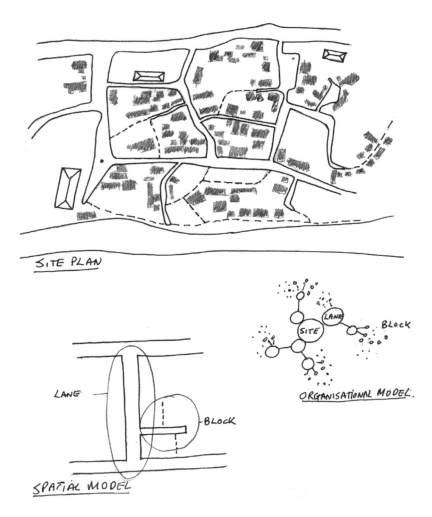

SITE PLAN

SPATIAL MODEL

LANE

BLOCK

ORGANISATIONAL MODEL.

SITE

LANE

BLOCK

Figure 7.5   *How spatial planning can mediate community organizing*
Source: Nabeel Hamdi

could have a say and more could get involved. We looked to organize
spatially by association with place rather than any other alliance and
would keep a careful watch on inclusivity and exclusivity. It would
be a rough breakdown to start with, fuzzy at the edges, but good

enough to get things going, to mobilize interest, build confidence and improve home life and street life.

As the diagrams above illustrate, we could model the site into lanes and clusters. Each cluster of some 30 families would elect a representative who would become a member of a lane committee (of which there may be five or six), responsible for broader issues of water, sanitation, waste management, security. Lanes would each, in turn, elect a representative to the Community Development Council (CDC) – the representative body whose responsibility it would be to advocate the community's case, to negotiate fair deals, with government and other authorities, to represent the community at Council meetings. Decisions would be taken at the level of clusters and lanes. Implementation and policy negotiation would be undertaken at the level of the CDC.

When it came to planning, we would start at the cluster and lane level, using a version of the process employed by Patama Roonrakwit in her settlement plans for the Under The Bridge dwellers in Bangkok: a series of parallel sessions in each of the clusters (some 30 in all over a period of two months) that we would jump-start with an example.[15]

In each cluster, families were asked to make a model of their homes and incorporate any aspirations they had for improvement or extension. They would, at first, be free to do this without the restriction of size of plots and with no worry about neighbours. Models could be made from anything and to a scale of about 1:50. Simple advice on scaling down (every step is one notch on a simple, made-up ruler) and on making models. Some used card and cloth and cans or plastic from bottles. Others used pastry and cookies – an invitation later to share in the culinary delights of their 'house cakes'. This process itself would generate substantial discussion among neighbours about ideas and techniques, each borrowing from the other. We would witness informal gatherings of an evening model making, some in the streets, some on roof terraces, others in houses.

When finally they brought their models to the workshop in our shed and outside among the knowledge fountains, they discussed their problems and ideals, at first individually then we would ask everyone to place their houses on a plan of the cluster and lanes that we had drawn and which filled the shed. There was at first the obvious confusion of whose plot was which and then, the confusion and disappointment of what it all looked like, when assembled. Those who had made additions would discover that they did not fit on their plot and began to encroach on neighbours. There were heated negotiations over boundaries, on privacy, on encroachment on to lanes without respect for setbacks. When, as in the example that Patama gives, everyone had agreed it was a mess, we began the process of drawing up a set of community derived standards that all would respect – simple at first, embellished later. Restrictions on plot boundaries, how much of your plot could be covered with building, setbacks from lanes, use of fronts, heights of buildings, positions of windows to avoid overlooking. Later, there would be agreement on tree planting in the lanes and even ideas on pooling resources for communal kitchens (to save space), for bulk purchasing of materials and on the collection and disposal of waste.

There would then be another planning workshop, for the site as a whole, this time between lane representatives. What would it all mean for lanes in terms of water, sanitation, waste management? Were the differentials in standards and aspirations between clusters acceptable? Did the differences matter? Were there standards or recommendations that all could share, which would give continuity and status to the settlement? And how did these relate to government standards for planning, for health and safety? What compromises would need to be negotiated? What changes would there have to be at the local level to conform, and at the urban level in order to enable upgrading that was affordable and yet acceptable? What standards or by-laws would have to be waived, and what precedent would this set for elsewhere? How much compliance and how much discretion? Why would it matter?

For the purpose of continuity, we would set up a 'Design Centre' at the shed and in close proximity to the recycling laboratory at the Urban Farm. It would be a drop-in centre for advice and ideas, manned mostly by students and volunteers doing fieldwork and getting experience. It would be managed in partnership with the CDC, the NGO and the University and overseen and partly funded by the municipalities' newly created Housing and Community Development Office. On its walls, all the community derived standards for planning and design, all the ideas for using waste and recycled materials for building, models and modelling materials you could work with in more detail for your improvements, and a whole site plan, tracking it all, as it emerged. There would be photographs of precedents and wider links to other projects with examples and ideas of what others have done worldwide.

HOMESTAYS

But how would the improvements be financed? There would be a block grant from the municipality, part of its Urban Regeneration Fund, directed at site level infrastructure improvements, including some money for public buildings, the shed, the Urban Farm and some general landscaping and investment in the improvement of markets, in particular along the waterfront. And then there would be collective saving and borrowing from each of the Lane Councils – who would become savings groups for their members and a part of the Urban Poor Fund Alliance with link-ups to the Women's Bank. Individual families would cluster as groups of 10–15 members and would secure loans for house improvements from either the Lane Council Fund or would form alliances with other groups facilitated directly by the Bank, and would become a branch of the Bank.

As we brainstormed alternatives someone, one of the young professionals in the group, came up with the idea of 'homestays' – places to stay in community for the adventurous tourist and, who knows, for those seeking 'boutique' alternatives! Given our location, it would generate income, improve the houses of those who wanted to join, raise the status of it all and source another pot of unlikely money for home improvements at least – from the National Tourist Board.

Some 40 families registered for the scheme. Each would receive a grant to bring their houses up to a standard of health and safety deemed appropriate by the Tourist Board. The group called themselves HOST (HOmeSTay). They would have to agree to regular inspections as a condition of the grant. Moreover, there would be a community contract issued to the Recycling Centre for furniture and fittings for each of the rooms, themed to attract the environmentally conscious visitor, with pictures and mirror frames made from tin, candlesticks of bottle tops and tuna tins, corrugated cardboard chairs, paper bowls for fruit, tables and beds from reused wood. One key area of concern where standards would be costly to meet was food hygiene when it came to kitchens and the preparation of food. HOST agreed to create a cooperative kitchen, extending the cafe at the Urban Farm as a restaurant for visitors. Organic food would be harvested from the shed's victory garden, installed as part of the knowledge centre, and from all the buffalo and mushroom produce at the Farm.

HOST Social Enterprises would receive training from the Tourist Board on food storage and preparation and food display, suitable and attractive to foreign visitors; and in bookkeeping and basic accounting from the Women's Bank. In addition, HOST would set up a reception centre for visitors, at the knowledge park: where to go, what was available, what you could expect during your stay. Room rates were set collectively. Money would be collected by each family, with an agreement to put 10 per cent into a collective fund for promotional material, for maintaining the reception centre and for occasional repairs and maintenance to members' houses.

HOST, like all the other initiatives at the Farm and elsewhere, would be scaled up over time, quantitatively in benefit, and scaled down progressively in ownership and control. They were scaled up functionally with all the integration, horizontally between locally based community groups, between those and other civil society groups, and vertically between these groups, and universities and government departments, and even global institutions. It was all scaled up politically, giving voice and authority to community organizations of varying sizes and organizationally in capacity and effectiveness. In time, it would all be an even more

wonderful place to grow up in.

In summary, if we track back and reflect on some of the principles driving our work, the list of recommendations might look something like this:

- start locally with problems, opportunities and aspirations and avoid convention (see Figure II.1, page 66);
- search out clues – local initiatives that you can build on and which can be a catalyst for change to improve life, livelihoods and the condition of place;
- reason backwards, from buffalos and mushrooms and getting to school, to enterprise and organization, from enterprise to community building, from community building to partnerships – to good governance and sustainable livelihoods – to meeting the Millennium Development Goals – to buffaloes and mushrooms and getting to school, globalizing the local and localizing the global, progressively and consistently;
- build local organization wherever possible – for enterprise, for planning, for management and savings;
- encourage networks, connecting as many of the initiatives as possible, adding social and economic value however seemingly unlikely;
- build community and all kinds of assets, through training, savings, enterprise, food production, going to school – networking, organizing and searching out partnerships;
- scaling it all up, progressively in benefit impact and network size, and scaling it all down in numbers, in control and responsibility, to safeguard ownership and ensure accountability;
- generate knowledge of place, in place, accessible and contestable, invoking corrections to our collective understanding of how things work;
- ensure that every step in planning is transformative, even the first, of place and of status, and that each intervention is visible and immediately recognizable in the benefits that it delivers;
- work with narrative, collect stories, start with aspiration, dream, imagine, and innovate, despite the constraints;
- with every practical intervention (improve houses for example) consider your strategic longer-term objectives and decide

further interventions, which you may need to achieve these (land markets, finance, tenure, voice, ownership);

- reflect progressively on rationale – what did you provide and enable, how did it adapt and transform and how will it be sustained (PEAS). What role and responsibilities did you assume, what constraints got in your way and how were they overcome? How was ownership cultivated and dependency reduced? What kind of learning did it inspire, and what difference will this make to your methods and routines (see Figure 11.1, page 171).

PART III
PLACEMAKERS:
RESPONSIBLE PRACTICE
AND THE QUESTION OF SCALE

The way of strategy lies in turning small things into big things. It is to have one thing and be able to do ten thousand things. It is like making a giant Buddha out of a one foot model. I cannot really explain how it is done.

Miyamoto Musaski
(16th-century Japanese strategist)

REFLECTION:
THE INVISIBLE STAKEHOLDER

We were doing street work for a community engagement project in the UK. The aim was to regenerate a busy high street to make it safer, less congested and a better environment for the community. Our task was to make sure the people living in the area had a say in the planning process and that their views and knowledge about the area were communicated effectively to the planners and engineers designing the scheme.

The tools and techniques of community participation we were using had been forged mostly in less developed countries. The planners and engineers raised eyebrows when we asked them to take part in think and listen sessions with community leaders, and ask schoolchildren to draw their ideas on maps of the area. We managed to convince the professionals that people in community have often some of the best ideas about what needs to happen to make a scheme successful.

We had taken over a disused shop in the area we were working in and had set it up as a drop in place for people to find out about the project. There was a window display of what we had done so far and the idea was people would come inside and take part in our participation events. The shop window worked well. It is worth remembering that you are up against a lot if you are trying to get people's attention to engage in your process.

One day I was outside the shop handing out fliers advertizing what we were doing, when a street person came up to me. It was cold that day, nearly Christmas. We were offering free tea, coffee and mince pies. He asked if he could come in for some tea and to get warm. I said yes, and suggested he might like to do some of our mapping activities too, which he did.

He stayed for a bit and had a look at what we were doing. He asked if there was anything he could do to help. I said he could hand out some fliers on the street. He willingly took on the task and before we knew it there were a good number of street people coming inside making their way to mince pies and hot drinks. All had been told, in no uncertain terms by our doorman, that yes they could come in and they would get free drinks and pies, but they had to take part in our information gathering activities, which they did. And we got fantastic information from a hard to reach group of rough sleepers in the community who we had identified as stakeholders, but had no idea about how we could engage with them.

The lesson I took away from that day was simple: be aware there are people out there you may not see, who are invisible as much to me as I to them. I might not know how to deal with them, or they might not be part of an identified stakeholder group, or they might cause conflict, or threaten me, or maybe hate me for what I am trying to do. I need to be flexible and aware enough to see an opportunity when it presents itself. One of my core practices in participation work, therefore, is to ask myself every day whether or not I am slipping back into my comfort zone, to check whether I am engaging with the whole community, not just talking to people I get along with, only the ones I find interesting, or who will give me answers I want to hear.

Charles Parrack

It was one of those 'break-out' sessions – break out, that is, from the captive and sometimes tedious drone of conference routine, following a presentation I had made on Community Action Planning. I was providing as examples some of the projects and programmes in which I have been involved, in India, Sri Lanka, South Africa, Peru and elsewhere. I was making my presentation to an audience of young professionals, in an attempt to demonstrate how process and product in participatory work, if done well, can liberate rather than confine the resourcefulness of people. In this sense, process can deliver both goods and services, and moral and social value as well.

'All well and good', someone said, 'but what does it all add up to in the longer term? Community Action Plans lack that bigger vision of city plans. They had failed to add up much, it seemed, in the context of the scale it all demands to engage with pressing global issues of poverty, rights and entitlements, the inequities of market protectionism and trade, of gender inequality, climate change, welfare aid and all the dependency it brings.' It was, indeed, a passionate plea from young professionals to find ways of getting engaged, of making a difference, in a world that had lost touch with its grass roots.

In the old days, one might have suggested we take to the streets with banners and loud speakers, or join some worthy cause to make our voices heard. But times have changed and so have tactics. My fellow break-outers were searching for ways to maintain a commitment to careers and the rigours of their disciplines, but in ways that would engage them as agents of change.

These questions sparked a wider discussion on how practical work can be scaled up in impact and made more strategic, and what kind of expert you have to be to do it all. Why do so many well-intentioned, even well-devised, projects and programmes fail to achieve a lasting impact in dealing with problems, and at a scale that counts? Why is it so difficult to sustain all the effort, to keep it all going long enough so that it can transform the lives and livelihoods of people and the fairness and safety of cities? What or who gets in our way and why?

In our continued discussions, critique from all those present was levelled in various ways: that scaling it all up demands the kind of money, institutional capacity and political good will that we rarely have; that the kind of change it all demands, in doing and thinking, in our relationships to people, are often threatening politically and professionally; that there is rarely coincidence between the social value of work and the economic demands of careers; that there is not enough learning as we go and, even when there is, it doesn't easily find its way back into practice to change the way we think and do; that corruption and greed take precedence over moral values, nearly always, so it seems; that we continue to tackle the symptoms of problems, leaving the longer-term systemic or primary causes for someone else to sort out – if at all, because we have timetables to stick to and fees to collect; and that, often, the solutions we devise to deal with problems that are often based on outsiders' priorities or agency mandates, induce partly other problems – the expulsion of people from urban land in favour of civic projects or Olympic villages in which we, the architects, planners and everyone else, are complicit.

Examples are plenty: '...the shift in funding focus from helping Kosovo Albanians just after the NATO [North Atlantic Treaty Organization] bombing, to supporting the return of Kosovo Serbs (in order to achieve the international objectives of a multi-ethnic society) increased inter-group animosity ... Their external agendas often set up perverse incentives. As one person said, "We asked for help for poor families that were not displaced, but we were told that this was not possible. We said, well what do we have to do to get assistance, leave Kosovo and come back again?"...'[1]

In another example, a worthy intent to promote ethnic inclusion and target multi-ethnic communities, exactly the opposite was achieved. 'To get aid', said one person, 'not only does your community have to have many ethnic groups, but they have to have problems with each other too!' In another community, people explained that they had a school, a health clinic and an electrical grid in their village, noting, 'We got all this aid because the village was multi-ethnic. The NGOs were fulfilling their own conditions. We heard this on TV.'[2]

And when we do attempt to deal with the underlying causes of problems, but when the going gets tricky for whatever reason, as it always does, we – the development practitioners – revert to generous but short-term tactics that we can measure or count to satisfy sponsors and our own need to achieve. We provide as much as we can that enables very little in the longer term – mosquito nets to fight malaria, houses to tackle housing, food parcels to tackle food security. None of these things builds assets in the long term. We revert, in other words, to palliative measures, 'Where the basic needs of the poor are taken care of, while the rest of the world gets on with its business.'[3]

In our examples at Thawra we saw how practical, basic needs interventions, if well placed and monitored, can start a process, which can deliver long-term value. We saw how small interventions can change the nature of place, cultivate community and, with it, the livelihoods and sense of belonging that comes with ownership. We saw how these processes can deliver all kinds of assets, locally and city-wide. Everywhere '...the contribution of millions of daily small actions by every individual, such as separating waste, thus brings about a great improvement in social productivity'.[4]

From these and all the other interventions designed as catalysts in the effort to get things going, and from my discussions with break-outers everywhere, I have begun to reflect more specifically on how the strategic value of small interventions can become more integral to Community Action Plans, rather than left somewhat to chance, while not ignoring that chance has a big role to play in planning ahead. From these discussions, I have begun to articulate, with friends and colleagues everywhere, what a Strategic Action Plan (SAP) looks like – what kinds of processes it implies, what kind of practices it demands and what kind of expert.

Two crosscutting themes recur in our search for method. The first is change – change in the way in which we reason practice and in the nature of professional conduct and responsibility. 'Change (however) only sticks when we have understood why it happened.'[5] Continuous change is, therefore, contingent on progressive learning.

Then there is change in place, the constant and progressive adaptations we make to our physical, social and economic environment, in order to maintain good fit and stability over time. This after all is the purpose of development. The capacity for this kind of change needs to be cultivated through design and good organization. It will demand a more flexible approach to the conventions of the project cycle (see Figure 9.2, Chapter 9) and to the standards and regulations, which get in the way. These kinds of change, in practice, in place and in the capacity of place to sustain change, are continuous and transformative.

The second crosscutting theme is scale – scale in numbers to meet demand and scale in impact of interventions. Going to scale is principally about mainstreaming – quantitively in programme size, logistics, money; functionally in the way in which programmes are integrated with other programmes or in the way in which organizations are federated city-wide, nationwide. Functionally also in partnership with private, government and non-government organizations, strengthening government and voluntary institutions; politically, in alternative forms of governance, more participation and the mediation of power relations; organizationally in leadership, in the capacity to scale up, in management capacity and in the skills and knowledge and institutional learning within organizations.

Change and scale are both explored in different ways in the following key components of Strategic Action Planning:

- in the conduct and responsibility of experts through what I have called PEAS;
- in the reasoning, and rationale of practice;
- in the management of constraints, to rights and entitlements for example and also programme constraints that inhibit innovation;
- learning and communication, about the growth and sharing of knowledge and experience and the importance of continuous reflection and feedback into practice; and in the dissemination of lessons learnt and the legibility of language and the media that we use;
- dependency and ownership – ownership of processes and of problems as well as solutions;
- sustaining livelihoods and reducing vulnerability – accumulating assets as a key objective of all interventions.

Too much forward reasoning, ignorance or the inability to manage constraints, an interruption to learning, poor communication, dependency-inducing behaviour or technologies, poverty and vulnerability, are all primary causes of problems we face in fieldwork cutting across housing, health, services and utilities. All are, therefore, integral to the planning of SAP.

8

PEAS AND THE SOCIABLE SIDE OF PRACTICE

First, we need to consider again the roles, responsibilities and obligations of experts and those whose duty of care extends beyond charity and into equitable and efficient design, city planning and urban management. When we reflect on the narrative and examples in Part II of this book and on other examples of CAP and participatory work worldwide, we begin to recognize (if not accept or assimilate) four integrally related sets of action vital to good development practice: Providing, Enabling, the capacity to be Adaptive, the capacity to Sustain (PEAS). Together, these define the ideals and activities of responsible practice.

PROVIDING

The first, providing, is easy to justify. It is what we as experts do best and what we were taught to do – to provide goods and services according to our expert skills and knowledge. When providing, however, is seen as an end objective and pursued as a discrete professional routine, then two things follow: either we retrench and slip back into top-down thinking and routine – we succumb to bad practice habits, and become antisocial; or we revert to charity.

In the first case, providing on its own imposes routines on practice, the kind that confine rather than liberate, creative work and the intelligence of place, when what we do and how we do it gets in the way of what we need to achieve.

At the heart of the dilemma is our own notion of what it takes to succeed as an expert – to be original, to defend your ground, to be rigorous, to be in control. We are driven by single solution thinking, by an obsession with excellence in search of definitive answers – getting it all 'generically right' in the interests of best practice, so that it can be replicated, and in pursuit of careers.[1] Our approach to problem seeking and to problem solving is linear and predictable: diagnose the problem, search out for opportunities, assess your risks, assemble the team, sort out budgets, draw up plans, design a response and deliver whatever. We relegate any participation we may be required to do into consultation at best, tokenism at worst.

We focus attention on 'things' and on making places, rather than on people, because people, we have decided, delay progress and clutter up the process. People, in any case, for most experts in the built environment at least, are someone else's problem. As a consequence, we impose a false divide between people and place. In so doing, we deny the role of place to mediate social and economic productivity. We deny the social equity principles of sustainable development, which demand an 'effective interlinked approach along social, environmental and economic domains at all spatial tiers of governance'.[2] We reinforce the strict boundaries that in the old days defined and protected professional domains. We compartmentalize problems to suit disciplinary skills, the way we were taught in schools, and place disciplinary skills into professional silos 'where planners operate in one sphere with their principles and maps, economists think about models, architects compete for design distinction – even while the challenges of today's cities cry out for collaborative approaches'.[3] Access to things (housing, schools, shops, playgrounds, toilets) takes precedence over access to opportunity. Our standards and planning laws, our housing estates and town plans confine and regulate more than liberate life chances.

And then we divide it all up again between those who make projects and those who devise policy, between both and yet others, the researchers and academics, the 'think tanks' and working groups whose job is to make sense of it all and sort things out.

When it comes to scaling it all up, for providers, this means building big and building more; and building faster means building all at once and in the shortest period of time. Timetables take precedence over life processes. Practice is simplified and reduced to a few safe and well-tried routines, so that it can be replicable. Everything is designed according to the ideals set by our profession and in search, forever, for perfection. All this in the interests of ensuring efficiency of systems and organization, and to justify interventions. 'If it were possible for bacteria to argue with each other, they would be able to say that of course their chief justification was the advancement of medical science!'[4]

The result: a false sense of quality in the exactness of plans and a bureaucratic dreamland of place and community. Worse still, a false sense of achievement among experts, a false sense of excellence. This 'relentless pursuit of excellence is the expert's badge of distinction'[5] and the trademark of providers. It is how we build our reputations and earn our status professionally. It is, however, an antisocial and self-deluding kind of expertise, because it breeds a false sense of self and, also, inequality between experts and non-experts. It alienates ordinary people and makes them feel stupid.

'I am convinced', says Ladislau Dowbor about the ways in which we organize and govern ourselves and the perfection and certainty we try to achieve, 'that today, the best approach [to getting relevant] is not another simplified certainty, but an open-minded approach of frank questioning, political creativity, tolerance and understanding. It is essential to keep the communication channels open between the various social sciences, between different types of institutions and between the range of organizing social players.'[6]

In cities everywhere, we have come to understand how intricate and complex formal and informal alliances and partnerships develop for building houses, managing waste, exchanging commodities, exerting rights and political advantages, securing employment, negotiating services and more. We have seen in time how people build their social networks and a substantial amount of knowledge, skills and experience about how best to build, to profit or dodge the authorities, despite all the constraints. When things go wrong, no one needs step in with elaborate explanations. People will visually have the know-how, if not the means or legitimacy to put it right. They will invent ways of working as they go, not always safely and not always fairly, but tailor-made to needs, income and sometimes even to aspirations. In all these respects, disciplinary silos, over-standardization and over-generalization denies the intelligence of informality and all the discretion it entails, because it threatens professional status and the perceived pursuits of excellence. Informality looks untidy and disorganized. The exactness of plans, whether for schools, housing or settlements, displaces the creativity of disorder in favour of places, which are easy to regulate and to manage by those who provide and others whose duty it is to implement policy. 'Nowhere in this view is serious thought given to how to capitalize on discretion as a device for improving the reliability and effectiveness of policies at the street level.'[7]

Over-regulation and over-standardization quickly become prescriptive and serve as a substitute for competence. They disturb the balance between design and emergence and with it the very people and organizations we now know are vital to the health and resilience of community. The opportunity of chance is denied, to be spontaneous, to improvise and to adapt in order to build and grow at a pace suitable to needs and capacities. 'Adaptation (of overly regulated plans) consist either of subversive, extra-legal behaviour, or a complex procedure of hierarchical clearance. There is little or no room for the exercise of special skills or judgement, not to mention deliberate intervention and experimentation.'[8]

The result is that people become dependent on having everything provided for them as commodity, including knowledge. 'The production of knowledge (when seen as a function of providing as a discrete routine) is inherently associated with current relations of power ... Knowledge serves the interests of control better than the needs of liberation. As such, knowledge itself becomes a repressive social force',[9] in particular when applied to the reasoning of exactness.

This reasoning when applied to placemaking and human development 'serves as a shield against exposure to others ... It is a borderline personality disorder arousing self-hate in ourselves as experts, because nothing is good enough, and humiliation and resentment in others.'[10] This antisocial expertise 'shames others and embattles or isolates experts'. You become your own critic forever searching for precedents of excellence devised by others, whether now or in history – a 'prisoner of envy'.[11] It doesn't take long to acknowledge your inability to be effective and subsequently to lose your self-respect.

What we get is a 'paralysis of the moral and political imagination'[12] because creativity and perfection become the mandate of the elite and gifted. The expert comes to be seen as a special kind of person, rather than that every person is a special kind of expert. Power relations are reinforced. All of which reflects in the behaviour and relationships to people who become beneficiaries rather than partners to our work.

We wind up diagnosing people and their condition of poverty, as if it were some kind of avoidable malignancy. (What you need to do is...) We contradict others who may not share our view of right or wrong, good or bad. We judge or stereotype those whose views and habits we find odd, but which may be entrenched in cultural norms and practices about which we may have, at best, a partial understanding. We will often label as troublemakers the loud or the pushy in community and so exclude the very people who can get things done. And because we are the experts, we wind up lecturing rather than dialoguing. When dialogue becomes monologue, we seed the beginnings of all kinds of social injustice.

We also become defensive. Our skills of defensiveness and manipulation have been developed over years of getting our own way, arguing our case in school project critiques or boardrooms – which are, in any case, confirmed by our international status. And when we can't get our own way, we wind up threatening and, in so doing, alienating again the very people and stakeholders whom we know we will need as partners, with whom we are purportedly participating. In all these respects, we are not good listeners because talking, not listening, is how you prove yourself – how you silence the opposition. It then follows, because we are not good listeners, we cannot be good learners – that sociable side of 'knowledge transfer rather than knowledge hoarding'.[13]

I started this chapter by suggesting that a second consequence of providing as a discrete routine is that it often becomes 'giving'. It becomes charity, driven by good intentions rather than informed priorities and often winds up 'more for the benefit of the giver than for the good of the recipient'.[14] D.H. Lawrence called this 'the greed of giving'. While charity at times of crisis is vital, it is nevertheless momentary, in particular when de-linked from PEAS. Providing as charity often embedded in relief aid, empowers celebrities 'who have become the face of Aid in Africa'.[15] The sentiment and guilt that often go with it all induce dependency and corrupt the moral high ground of good governance.

Governments come to rely on outsiders to deal with health, education, poverty and crises, while they pursue other goals, however legitimate. Charitable interventions are mostly piecemeal and rarely sustainable. And when they are tied to conditionality, governments become responsible to donors and celebrities rather than their own people. When de-linked to each of the other components of PEAS, providing as charity induces a moral superiority among providers. 'It can become an important drive and even a sickness in which they (the providers) urgently need the continuing contact with recipients to give added meaning to their lives. Helping becomes a drug ... We need to protect others and ourselves from the consequences of good intentions ... When good intentions are entangled with feelings of moral superiority, it can be twice as dangerous. This mixture can encourage the recipient to feel worthless and third rate; seeing us as "good" and himself as "bad". It is so much harder to struggle against the pressing attentions of someone who is intent on undermining you by doing good.'[16]

ENABLING

Those by now, who know the limitations of providing, have sought to reposition themselves as enablers. This either–or distinction is neither helpful nor accurate. I have come to believe that in order to be an effective enabler, you have to be a prudent provider. The value of providing in this case is partly measured in its own right (the buffalo, the mobile unit, micro finance, the house, the water tap) in the practical way in which it meets the needs of now and, significantly, in the way in which it enables others to provide for themselves, to build assets now or soon and later.

I take enablement to mean the ability or willingness to provide the means with which to open doors and create opportunities in order to build livelihoods, reduce vulnerability and sustain development. As such, and despite the wrath of neo-liberal labelling, enablement, as we have seen it practised in our examples, cuts across all three of Burgess' distinctions.[17] With community enablement, the focus is clearly on people and on building their capacity to be recognized as the mainstream, rather than a social or economic liability; political enablement is the strategic task of all Development Practice – to influence policy, change standards, remove discrimination, promote rights and open doors. And market enablement because opening up markets for small-scale social enterprise both in terms of skill, produce and products is a part of sustaining community. It is integral to our definition of good governance. And rather than deny the state its role, it realigns the state and the formal market in partnership with civil society.

Critique and debate over the advantages and consequences of enablement are well analysed by Burgess, Carmona and Kolstee. In practice and for the development practitioner, however, with enablement comes a very different set of values, tools, skills, methods and relationships to partners and project work. It gets us involved in products and activities we may not conventionally see as part of our disciplinary work, certainly not as providers – as we have witnessed in our case examples. Building organizations, for example, conflict resolution negotiation skills, innovating with partnerships. It demands entrepreneurship and all the spontaneity of spotting and building on opportunities, as you go. Then there are all the training and capacity building activities, the participatory tools of role play and gaming. When it comes to outputs, we find ourselves designing games for groups to play in order to inform and to socialize – board games, or planning kits, or card packs. Our models of houses or schools or playgrounds are interactive rather than representational, again to inform and promote discovery of different ways to lay out a plan or use a building. Then there may be handbooks and manuals to guide the design implementation or management of projects and programmes, to explore alternatives that capture local wisdom and local knowledge. Many of these emerge during project work. In other words, the people involved contribute to and sometimes lead in the design of these tools.

But it is all contingent on what we provide, a check on how much we should provide – catalysts rather than projects, starting points not end states. It all depends on what you have got locally in resources, on conditions and circumstances on the ground. In these ways, design and planning become themselves a process of enablement, cultivating place in ways that liberate the resourcefulness of people, always adaptive and transformative.

ADAPTABILITY

Which leads us to the third component of PEAS: adaptability and change. How should we think about change and resilience as integral to planning and design? How should we go about making matters imprecise[18] in order to invite change? We know that the capacity for change is a resource with which to sustain well-being, build community and a sense of belonging and identity. It is a resource for building all kinds of assets, tangible and intangible. But what does it mean for planning and design and for placemaking?

Change is still seen today as a threat to the precision of planning. It is interference to well-rationalized plans, a threat rather than a corrective to the status quo, of professional responsibilities. Change and adaptation invoke a natural and inclusive process of incremental adjustments to ensure good fit over time. John Habraken, in his book *Palladio's Children* recalls about architects: '...In mainstream design, growth and change stimulate little creative thinking or recognition as a source of inspiration leading to a new architecture ... The large-scale project must intrinsically sustain partial or uneven change over time if it is to both shelter and sustain small-scale life ... Our instinct is to defy time and to preserve what we have wrought. The special building – the villa, the palace, the castle, the house of worship – is intended to be immutable in the steadily transforming field: a stone in running water.'[19]

In summary in order to change to fit, then places must be made fit for change. But how should we go about doing this?

In his exploration of an alternative architecture, Colin Ward identified a number of themes, linked by their intent to explore change as a way of disciplining design and planning.[20] He refers to the infinite variability of the vernacular of anywhere, both formal and informal, as it adapts to the needs of time and aspiration with minimum waste. He writes of the ecological impulse, with its desire for long-life, low-energy, loose fit – where autonomy and self-sufficiency drive the search for an architecture of good fit, between both the natural and built environment. Then there was his adaptive or 'convivial' alternative – convivial in Illich's terms because it gives a maximum of opportunity for people, not experts, to stamp their own visions and identities on place, rather than 'allow the designer to determine the meaning and expectations of others'. This, he wrote, relegates people to the subservient role of 'caretaker', 'because the greater the expertise, the power and status of a profession, the smaller the opportunity for the citizen to make decisions'. Ward reminds us of his three gurus of modern town planning: Howard, Geddes and Kropotkin. All viewed planning '...not as a profession nor a body of legislation, but as a popular movement, a public enthusiasm, part of the social economy'.

Ward's fifth alternative recalled the writings of Simon Nicholson and his theory of loose parts. 'In any environment, both the degree of inventiveness and creativity, and the possibilities for discovery are directly proportional to the number and kind of variables in it.'[21] These variables offer both clarity of opportunity and yet an indeterminacy about ends. They offer an acceptable degree of tolerance or variation in meaning, or in value and function.

Ward's themes offer a basis for thinking afresh the placemaker's art. They lead us to think of design and planning not as a process, which necessarily produces an architecture of building. Nor does it produce the conventional site plan with its neat lines, and distinct and colourful depiction of function, circulation patterns and public open spaces. 'It will not seek to designate a discrete "end state" for the simple reason that there is none; and it will not be based on zoning regulations and density standards, since the aim is to create conditions and not impose restrictions.'[22] Rather, it represents an architecture of invitation and of opportunity, with some formal modelling, with roads and pathways, parcels and lots, all of which may well be annotated with light, shade, trees, boundaries, barriers, utilities and differential lot sizes and land values.

As we have seen in our examples in Part II, the plan is not some sacred prototype to be tested in its compliance with preordained rules. Neither was the design process concerned only with problem solving, in the sense that a solution is expected to emerge at the end. Rather, the plan, in its structure and arrangement is an expression of shared aspirations and an expression of creative opportunities. It represents 'a minimum of organization that would serve the benefits of planning, while leaving individuals the greatest possible control over their own lives'. Its aims: '...to sustain as many particularities as possible, in the hope that most people will accept, discover, or devise one that fits'.[23] The plan, with its rules, opportunities and constraints, serves legibly as a chessboard might to a chess player. As Habraken put it:

> The basic exercise gives us the ingredients of a design attitude. We see in the form at hand, the moves available to us. We enter into a dialogue with the form. Our freedom is in choosing the next move; our skill is in choosing what leads us in the general direction we must take to satisfy a demand or a strategy. Our knowledge and experience lie in being able to find many alternative moves. The result of such humble beginnings, if the process is continued, can be very complex and very rich.[24]

What we get, as a result and in summary, is a science of the everyday based on the following:

- the capacity or tolerance of place for change;
- the legibility of place – with space for human development and well-being;
- the accommodation of difference – an invitation to differentiate and at the same time to assimilate;

- the indeterminacy of content – and initial ambiguity of meaning that will become purposeful and meaningful during habitation.

SUSTAINABILITY

Some time ago, on one of those looking and listening phases of fieldwork, I became intrigued with shop signage: in particular, signs that define what shop owners provide and also what they aspire for their customers. It was a place that we were visiting with all kinds of beauty parlours, hairdressers and tailors: 'Gloria's Head for Heights'; 'Head Shine and Shoe Shine – we work at both ends'; 'Jackets and Dreams – the tailor of cool' and others. One sign particularly attracted my attention: 'The Sustainable Barber's Shop'.

We went in to talk to the owner to find out what was meant. The barber was a young man in his twenties, a graduate of technical college but who had started his own part-time business, with his father, cutting hair. When we asked for his meaning of sustainability, I had half expected some version of the widely read Brandt Report, or to be impressed with his recycling of grey water, his solar driven razors or all the other gizmos that would save the world. Instead, his own version was more pragmatic. 'When my customers come in', he said, 'I cut enough hair to satisfy their needs and aspirations for now, but not too much, so that they come back sooner rather than later. That way, I keep my business going.'

Sustainability, the fourth component of PEAS, is by now already largely defined, implicit in all of PEAS: the importance of providing catalysts and the many forms this can take, physical, spatial, monetary or indeed in services and capacity building. There are the responsibilities and activities of enablers in promoting community enablement, as well as market and political enablement, all of which sustain progress and multiply opportunity. Then there is the capacity for change that 'after all is only another word for growth, another synonym for learning', that ability to be adaptive socially and spatially, to build resilience and to sustain development. All these define a culture of practice, both practical in its objectives, and strategic in its purpose, with a strong commitment from all 'to share in the responsibility for the future, which begins now'.[25] Being strategic is synonymous with being sustainable. Sustainability both derives from these themes and is a check on their value over time, widening opportunity and promoting a lasting impact. This lasting impact we will see in subsequent chapters is contingent on dealing with the primary causes of problems, as outlined at the start.

First, however, when we provide in order to enable, when we enable to adapt or when we provide, enable and adapt in order to sustain, we invoke a way of reasoning and a rationale for work, which is anti-convention. It demands a change in process, no less than a change in the logic of project work.

9

REASONING TO SCALE

Much of the rationale of Strategic Action Planning (SAP) is already implicit in PEAS. Also implicit is the action science reasoning that underpins all Action Planning, both CAP (Community Action Planning) and SAP.

The objectives of CAP and SAP are illustrated and compared in the figure below. Together, they give purpose to practice beyond just practical work, a commitment to structural and not just remedial change, in the interests of lasting development.

CAP	SAP
Timescale (now, soon)	Timescale (soon, later)
Access to shelter/services/utilities	Access to resources, removing constraints, power sharing
Problem solving	Rights, entitlements Discrimination
Plans, projects, programmes	Policies, standards legislation, institutional reform, partnerships
Outputs (quantitative) – houses, water, etc	Outcomes (qualitative) – well-being, livelihoods security
Good practice (local)	Good principles (transferable)
Small scale project based	Large scale, urban/national scaling up, quantitatively, functionally, politically, organizationally

Figure 9.1 *CAP and SAP: comparative and complementary objectives*
Source: Nabeel Hamdi

In this chapter, I will explore some of the important synergies between CAP and SAP, those that distinguish their routine and purpose from the conventions of logical framework analysis. I will argue the need for synergy between the logic of forward planning implicit in log framework analysis and that of backward reasoning implicit in all action planning. Each of the processes is distinguishable in their logic and reasoning; in their organization (the first hierarchal in relationships and decision making, the second more networked); and in process (in the sequence of steps each adopts when defining objectives, deciding interventions and formulating policy). How might we converge the value of both logical framework analysis with its propensity to plan forwards and SAP? Can the ideals and aspirations of a sustainable development coincide with the pragmatism of delivering aid and programmes when and where they count most?

For pragmatists, two themes are dominant when searching for method. The first, the need for more cooperation among partners, in particular with civil society groups – in pursuit of good governance. The second, improved coordination of effort among all stakeholders. The overriding and agreed objective is to improve the efficiency of aid delivery, while ensuring transparency and accountability. Reducing waste in effort and money and targeting interventions more effectively are key objectives to scaling up effort and impact in whichever way you reason your planning.

Cooperation is about partnerships, sometimes formal, sometimes informal. It's about coming to consensus about a common goal, recognizing that no one partner alone can achieve. It's about participation and shared responsibility, consolidating rights and deciding obligations.

Underlying the concept of cooperation and partnership are two defining considerations: mutuality and identity.[1] Mutuality entails cooperation between stakeholders, creating an environment in which talents, skills or know-how are valued and exchanged among partners for the benefit of all. Mutuality builds on strengths. It accepts that all parties, however unequal in experience, talent or power, represent an asset. Mutuality 'moves relationships from a hierarchal state of dependence and independence toward one that is horizontal and interdependent'.[2] It is in this respect that forward reasoning is critiqued, given its hierarchal order of decision making.

The second consideration is identity – the kind of identity that ensures both distinction and legitimacy. 'The creation and maintenance of organizational identity is essential for longer term success',[3] for sustaining progress. Brinkenhoff suggests two levels at which identity needs to be examined and defined. First, the collective identity that comes with a commitment to goals set collectively. Second, the identity of each individual constituent, whose expertise, skills and codes of conduct enable them to be both distinctive from, yet integral to, the whole. The loss of individual distinction often leads to dependence; the loss of commitment to the whole leads to competition and undermines the value of partnership.

Close on the heels of cooperation comes the demand for better coordination of effort, providing coherence in planning and continuity when all the outsiders have left. It is reasonable to assume that you cannot easily coordinate the efforts of partners who do not want to cooperate, or who have decided that cooperation interferes with individual partners' agendas or identity. While cooperation is about comparative advantage and risk, about trust and finding the common ground in respect to ideals and expectations, in goals and objectives, coordination is about technique, information, logistics and efficiency of effort. It is about coherence and preparedness. But what kind of coherence? It is here, where the rationale of forward reasoning differs significantly from backward reasoning, and why each in their own right is incomplete in so far as planning processes are concerned.

Coherence conventionally and when reasoning forwards is guided by the kind of rationale that is logical, consistent, free of ambiguity, precise. It demands, as a measure of the effectiveness, that all the pieces of any plan fit neatly together – where every step you take is explainable in terms of the last step you took and the next one you have to take.

Forward reasoning begins at the top of the planning process with a clear statement of purpose or policy, derived typically from a global understanding of big issues, which it then attempts to localize. It outlines specific objectives, which programmes will achieve, and a series of equally specific steps of how they will be achieved. It will define the outputs at the bottom of the sequence, and also how they will be measured. As a part of the planning and implementation process, roles and responsibilities of various actors will be outlined, often more precisely than is realistic, at least at the planning stage. Relationships between the various government and non-government organizations will often be mapped, as will the anticipated relationships with civil society groups and private sector ones as well. Measurable indicators of progress and achievement will also be articulated, preferably in ways that are observable and quantifiable. At each stage, risks or assumptions are made clear in relation, for example, to political viability or to the application of some new and desired technology.

On its own, forward reasoning with its logic of coherence, is problematic in various ways. It reinforces the myth that practice can be controlled from the top, because that's where it starts, driven by experts whose business it is to ensure compliance with national and international norms and standards, agreed globally. It assumes that policymakers are adequately equipped or even well enough informed about the appropriateness of policy in the mess of practice. Its tendency is to assume normative standards of correctness or success. It is the logic and reasoning of providers, de-linked from PEAS, top down in bias, working often from the outside in.

My own view is less that this kind of reasoning is deficient in its own right, but rather that it is incomplete as a process for placemaking and human development. It is inadequate as a tool for the development practitioner, instrumental at best, coercive at worst. The 'tight fit' coherence it demands interrupts performance because performance in the mess and uncertainty of the everyday demand that we 'befriend ambiguity'.[4] Ambiguity and uncertainty guard against error. They encourage enquiry and therefore a deeper understanding of place. Ambiguity and uncertainty demand discretion and flexibility – that ability to improvise and tap your intuition, your wisdom and those of others, as your stumble on advantages and opportunity. Coherence of this kind and all the compliances it demands is what gives us our master plans and housing estates. It distorts the real and renders buildings and place lifeless under the guise of equity, security or efficiency of output. It is hierarchal in organization and in relationships.

> ... *the closer one is to the source of the policy, the greater is one's authority and influence; and the ability of complex systems to respond to problems depends on the establishment of clear lines of authority and control. Backward (reasoning) assumes essentially the opposite: the closer one is to the source of the problem, the greater is one's ability to influence it; and the problem-solving ability of complex systems depends not on hierarchal control but on maximizing discretion at the point where the problem is most immediate.* [5]

Or at the point where the opportunity is most evident.

In this respect at least, backward reasoning is a corrective, not a substitute for forward planning. It is a corrective to the control imposed by hierarchy and by those at the top who decide policy. It also subscribes to coherence, but not the coherence of sameness or tight fit. Instead, it is the coherence of difference and loose fit. It is the coherence of ambiguity rather than precision, where each step you take and each intervention you make tells something about the next.

Reasoning backwards assumes that processes of implementation, for housing, services and utilities for building communities and securing rights are on going and integral to any future planning. It assumes that good policy, responsible design and good planning derive from good practice reasoned backwards from consequence to effect to cause and then to plans. It starts, therefore, at the bottom of the planning process. It starts with looking and listening, describing problems and opportunities, capturing aspirations, exploring the behaviour of organizations on the ground and the interactions of social or other networks. Only then does the process attempt to state objectives, and it does so with all those who are closely associated with or affected by problems, who may be individual households, community-based organizations (CBOs), enterprises or government bodies. Once these objectives have been prioritized and agreed, only then does the analysis 'back-up' into implications for policy or for appropriate technologies or the need for specialized skills or knowledge. This leads us to craft policies and plans, which may be seemingly inelegant, and yet are often 'good enough' for purpose, with less waste. What we get is a larger ordering framework of policies and standards, which will have more chance of 'buy-in' because most people and organizations on the ground will have contributed to their emergence and construction.

Backward reasoning takes ideas, habits, conventional wisdoms, lessons from the everyday in order to inform behaviour and policy globally.

> *[It] shares with forward [reasoning] the notion that policy makers have a strong interest in affecting the implementation process and the outcome of policy decisions. But backward [reasoning] explicitly questions the assumption that policy makers ought to, or do, exercise the determinant influence over what happens in the implementation process. It also questions the assumptions that explicit policy directives, clear statements of administrative responsibility, and well-defined outcomes will necessarily increase the likelihood that policies will be successfully implemented ... [Backward reasoning] offers instead a standard of success that is in all respects conditional: that is, ones definition of success is predicated on an estimate of the limited ability of actors at one level of the implementation process to influence the behaviour of actors at other levels, and on the limited ability of public organizations as a whole to influence private behaviour.*[6]

If we now refer to Figure 9.2, we can see how both routines can work in synergy, delivering practical interventions reasoned from the street and informing longer-term strategic advantage.

Two characteristics are worth noting. First, the cycle of planning is reversed. Rather than start with policy and move down to projects, we start with projects, a series of catalyst interventions to improve conditions locally. These catalysts help to shape the larger urban plan. They are its molecular structure, its DNA and give it its character and coherence. These urban plans are the basis for policymaking. As we feed the policies back into practical work, as we attempt to localize each in practice, we can review the extent to which problems have been solved and opportunities cultivated. And so again, the cycle of setting new objectives, of continuously

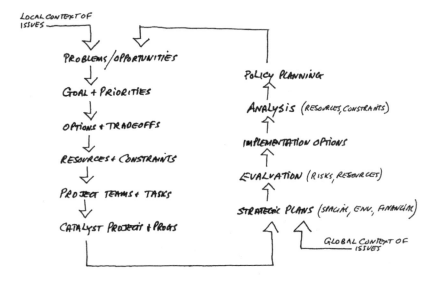

Figure 9.2 *Completing the project cycle – CAP and SAP*
Source: Nabeel Hamdi

re-prioritizing, of looking at resources and evaluating constraints, identifies more catalyst projects, continuously.

Many of the successful examples we have visited so far in this book have followed this road map. The Women's Bank, for example, which emerged from needs defined locally, with its catalysts of small savings groups, branch organization and training. Later the federation of these small groups that through progressive analysis of effectiveness, backed by new government policy, enabled it to flourish. Policies for credit and new partnerships were continuously scaled down and evaluated in terms of their local effectiveness at delivering benefits. Pooja's latrines tell a similar story, and so do the homestays in our example in Part II. The need for improved housing, the catalyst of homestays, the larger city plan for tourism that emerged, the shift in standards and policy by the tourist board that made it happen and grow, the improvement of houses, the opportunity to generate income and so on.

The second, and by now obvious characteristic of the diagram, is the essential proximity that it crafts between policy planning and project planning: the first, responding to urban and national priorities, the second to local needs. Both policymaking and problem solving are at the top of the diagram and in direct relationship. Policymakers are therefore placed closer to the problems that they are mandated to solve; and project makers, including community, through their actions are better integrated into urban planning and policy development. In all these ways, reasoning backwards, completing the loop progressively and collaboratively improves performance and unblocks learning.

Despite all this, there will of course remain constraints to building this new road map and shifting conventions of planning routine. Some we have already explored (the dominance of hierarchy, the pervasiveness of experts). Others are more programmatic – institutional capacity, lack of money, lack of political goodwill, for example. In the following chapter, we explore one further set of constraints: those imposed by the limits of our own expectations as experts of what we can or should achieve – and the problems we choose to engage.

10

TARGETING CONSTRAINTS

The way in which we manage or manipulate constraints in project design can either control or unlock creative work.

Rules, regulations and accepted cultural norms offer us codes of social, cultural and technical conduct that determine, in part, the limits to which we are expected to adhere and, subsequently, the freedoms we enjoy professionally and as citizens. This constantly shifting relationship between freedom and order, between those structures by design and those that are emergent has been a dominant theme among social scientists, economists, planners and architects.[1]

In 1975, Christopher Alexander in his book *The Oregon Experiment* said, 'Many of the most wonderful places in the world, now avidly photographed by architects, were not designed by architects but by lay people. But of course, in order to create order, not chaos, people must have some shared principles. Nothing would be worse than an environment in which each square foot was designed according to entirely difference principles. This would be chaos indeed.' He went on to explore his 'pattern language' – a language of rules and relationships between the physical and spatial make-up of place, open to interpretation and modification. 'These patterns give the user a solid base for their design decisions. Each person, or group of people, will be able to make unique places, but always within the morphological framework created by the pattern.'[2]

But how are these patterns devised, by whom and with whom? What if they get in the way of innovations and interfere with the freedom to find unique expression or to sustain livelihoods? What if they are purposely designed to suppress rather than liberate? Changing the rules, managing the constraints, rewriting codes of conduct, are the most profound strategic interventions one can make, whether these rules govern habit, ritual or routine. Changing the rules, after all, changes the conduct of work, not just work itself. It both liberates and limits opportunity in an ever-changing relationship. When limits become barriers, when precedent can no longer justify decisions to meet new goals in times of discontinuous change – to deal with climate change or the unprecedented growth of cities – then new limits have to be negotiated. That, after all, is the purpose of participation in planning, and at the core of democratizing governance.

Two sets of constraints need constant review and adjustment. The first are in respect to the limits of our own professional aspirations and expectations of what we should or are able to achieve, given our understanding of context. The second set of constraints are those that have become embedded in our standards, laws, regulations, for whatever reason, and places, limits on access to essential resources to meet basic needs, for people to exercise their rights. Most are discriminatory. This second set we will return to in Chapter 13 on livelihoods.

First, however, how should we unravel the limits of our own expectations, given all there is that will block our way to achieving objectives?

My findings, over the years, have led me to conclude the following: there are things you should do but can't, given all the programmatic constraints every time you start. Some constraints on our professional expectations will be technical in nature – issues of time and logistics, of availability of materials or appropriate technologies – getting the right information, respecting the vernacular, and some will be financial. There will be institutional constraints around issues of capacity or status, the lack of inter-agency cooperation, or institutional transparency and accountability, constraints on new partnerships or better ways of organizing to improve the design, implementation and management of programmes. Then there will be constraints imposed by politics – locally, nationally, globally. There will be community organizations who themselves will be vying for power or status, and other leaders who may be on your side but who will shift ground for political expediency rather than need. Political constraints will be extreme in areas of ongoing conflict, or where political advantage after disasters takes precedence over rational choice or local need. Witness the problem of reconstruction post-tsunami everywhere.[3]

Then there are things you don't do because you don't know how, you don't have the experience or knowledge, or because it's not your mandate or priority – but should be. There are other things you shouldn't do but still do because lessons haven't been learnt, because that's what is expected of you, that's what you are paid to do – that's what you have been doing all your professional life – your career depends on it. And finally, there are things you don't even think about – not just because you don't know but also because you have decided it's not your business or responsibility – you think – although maybe it should be.

Juggling all the positions every time we are faced with the design or planning of a placemaking project or programme, at least one with 'development' objectives, induces quite often guilt, resentment, a sense of hopelessness and pessimism about our ability to change worlds. In the interconnectedness of global issues and responsibilities today, you come to realize that you can't do one thing without dealing with everything and everything, which you know is impossible to do. As a result, our competence or professionalism is brought in to question and our engagement with issues that matter is often undermined and so, therefore, is our self-respect. We wind up doing projects where we know we can succeed, where it's not too difficult, not too problematic and, often, not too important. We stick to the safe ground and limit our ability to innovate. Failure, we know, is unacceptable because it threatens our identity and reputation. Getting it wrong is not, in the eyes of our public institutions, a part of getting it right.[4] Learning and innovation are interrupted and set aside in favour of careers and other ideals. Mistrust, defensiveness, jargon, abstraction and intellectual competition compound our alienation from the everyday.

Most constraints, of the kind I have mapped, are conventionally about 'can't'. They are seen to get in the way of what we want to do. They threaten the success or status of our project and programme – success that is according to agendas and criteria that are set by our professional or global institutions, which are always difficult to localize without big changes. And so we wind up doing less than we had intended or know is right. We de-link what we do – build houses, latrines, roads, schools – from what we know we should also do – build a sense of belonging, turn favours or gifts into entitlements, ensure rights, improve governance, reduce vulnerability. We isolate things, techniques and technologies from life values, which, once again, render our work instrumental at best. The result: we wind up doing a lot, seemingly, but achieving very little because we subjugate our moral responsibilities in favour of corporate or professional or other interests over those of people. David Korten in his book *The Post Corporate World* sums it up neatly:

> *When the modern corporation brings together the power of modern technology and the power of the great mass of capital, it also brings in the scientist (planner, architect, engineer) whose self-perception of moral responsibility is limited to advancing objective instrumental knowledge, and the corporate executive whose self-perception of moral responsibility is limited to maximizing profit. The result is a system in which power and expertise are delinked from moral accountability, instrumental and financial values override life values, and what is expedient and profitable takes precedence over what is nurturing and responsible.*[5]

In response to the above, three more things to think about: first, I tend to assume that many of the constraints we confront in the mess of practice are a context for work rather than a barrier to it. While I may not accept that context to be legitimate or morally acceptable, and while in the longer term I will know that the context itself is one of the primary causes of many of the problems that will need tackling, it is, nevertheless, my starting point. I accept, for now, that some of these constraints will remain unresolved. In the interest of my own self-care I will have to change my expectation of how much I can achieve. This determines how much I can do today, how far I can go and where I can start. One only need observe the creativity of many of the poorest, to wonder at their ability to manoeuvre within the appalling constraints imposed by poverty, to realize that this first axiom of practice has value.

Second, I measure my progress and success in my ability to open doors to get things going and then the entrepreneurship that it takes to keep it going – and not in the requisite quite often of my sponsors to 'deliver' on projects. In other words, I seek to find an intervention, however small, which can serve as a catalyst for achieving longer term more strategic objectives, to tackle constraints and scale it all up. Very few of these catalysts would have been invented before work starts. Rather, they are sought out on location, opportunities you look out for and stumble upon – the pickle jar, the bus stop, the buffalo, mushrooms, the homestay, the piedibus – which, when reasoned backwards, become places and organizations of pride and dignity.

All of this gets you involved, very often, in things you don't normally do or intended to do but have to, and other things you know you shouldn't do but do anyway to get jobs started. It gets you focused on pursuing ideals, not just project objectives.

Take for example our arrival 'in community' at Santay Island, Ecuador by naval gunboat. We all knew this was bad practice as an entry into participation with the islanders but the navy held a significant base on the island. It was a reminder of who was in control and of the stake they had in any negotiations on the future of the island. And yet our arrival in this way signalled our alliance with the navy – an obvious bias in favour of their demands – a bad start in our deliberations with community. And yet working with the 'bad guys' sometimes opens doors for the 'good guys'.

Then there were the negotiations over debt transfer with both the British and Ecuadorian governments – a way of using debt toward a worthy project, in this case the environmental protection of Santay. None of us knew much about the debt transfer scheme but it didn't take long to grasp the essentials. But was this our mandate or responsibility?

How do you advise an NGO tempted with a US$20 million donation for building shelter for the poor in Israel on condition they dropped their operations in Egypt, which in any case were small? Or the fieldworker whose shelter programme in Bosnia for people displaced after the conflict would depend first on providing a Palladian villa for the government official in charge? Would it be good practice to do so and benefit hundreds of families, or bad ethics?

In these and many other cases, we are always faced with contemplating the legitimate boundaries of our expertise and what is morally acceptable – that fine line between being ethical or otherwise. Should we or shouldn't we? It's the kind of debate that is rarely conclusive in the absence of context, except in the most general way. Or, as I have tended to do, you can ignore the debate and focus instead on what you need to do to be relevant, to make a difference, without losing your self-respect.

Third, and in response to constraints self-imposed by habit when formulating a programme of work, I start the project with what is feasible, although it may not always be technically logical. I start with what everyone has agreed are priorities, with problems we share or that unite rather than those that divide. Starting and in the process resolving conflict 'acting to induce others to act' helps build cooperation among sometimes unlikely partners (the navy and the community) exposing where we disagree, as a vehicle for understanding differences rather than being threatened by them. In this way, we 'dance with conflict'[6] as a way of orchestrating the way forward. We avoid getting it all sorted before we start because starting is a vehicle for getting it sorted – in the process.

In 1994, the apartheid regime in South Africa was finally dismantled. Not long after, the government published its famous Reconstruction and Development Program (RDP) report – a document we had all wished we had written – championing the cause of civil society and, in its own words, good governance and sustainable development. We had secured a grant from the Overseas Development Administration (ODA) to explore the potential for Community Action Planning as a way of starting the process of integration between townships and town – to begin at least a process of building cooperation.[7]

On the third day of our planning workshop, we were interrupted by a group of people claiming the right to be involved. They had gatecrashed the workshop because they had not been included as legitimate participants. It turned out that they were members of a communist elite, a stark reminder of power divisions within the townships in which we had assumed homogeneity.

One way, of course, to avoid interruptions would have been to bar them entry to the proceedings – to exclude, as one is always tempted to do, the troublemakers. But troublemakers are an important source of information – people who often have a counter view to the mainstream and can offer creative alternatives. Listening to the strongest part of their case, not the weakest, can be productive and inclusive. In any case, to exclude them would have involved open conflict. We were there to build bridges, not to emphasize divisions.

We embarked upon a version of that routine in Planning for Real, where everyone writes down, anonymously, a priority concern and places it on a map of the area. It is an exercise where the focus of attention is where you live and work rather than at the committee table. It avoids the eyeball to eyeball negotiation where people argue their cause and become defensive, or where status counts more in winning your point than actual need.

In our case, each of the now 40 or so individuals wrote a single priority issue and set it out on the floor. Everyone circulated and read each card. If it didn't match their priority, they turned it over. Once turned, you could look to see what is said, but you had to keep it turned. Of the 40 or so cards, two remained unturned – two issues that, therefore, everyone either agreed was a priority or it didn't really matter to them either way. The first reflected the need for a bus or other transportation service to get the elderly from one end of town to the clinic that was situated at the other end. The second was the need to put in street lights. The existing lights – which at first seemed adequate to us – resembled those floodlights that you see around the perimeters of prisons: to keep people in or, in this case, to give the old guard police easy and visible access in case of trouble. The lights were symbolic of a time now passed.

Our first response was to look at all the cards turned over and freak out! To start a discussion where there was disagreement – a sure recipe for more conflict and division. Instead, we took the two issues about which at least there was no objection and looked for solutions. We started where it was feasible and not necessarily logical in terms of planning routine or log framework analysis, which opened doors to progressing work towards resolving other issues of concern (not only the symptoms but the primary causes themselves) over the longer term. As Mark Napier reported on the workshop in 1995:

> ...And so the process carries on for four days – huddle, present, huddle, agonize, re-think, present, re-work, re-present – until gradually the action plans take shape ... Without losing sight of the larger needs, ways are devised of chipping away at the huge block of initial hopelessness: schemes in which community plumbers form teams that fix leaking water pipes, plans for longer working hours and better staffing at the clinic, better sanitation practices, job creation projects, improvements to building materials supplies, and better access to building skills and training ... without fanfare and almost unnoticed, a small group of community leaders and representatives have been given a vision of what their neighbourhood could look like, and have been empowered to begin realising some parts of that dream.[8]

11

LEARNING AND COMMUNICATION

One of the biggest constraints to change is our lack of willingness or capacity to learn, because we don't have the time or because we think we already know what needs to be known to get the job done – or because it's someone else's business. This reliance on others to generate knowledge and find answers, the researchers and academics, encourages more divisions between those who do and those who think, which makes the assimilation of learning more difficult. Learning is 'a growth of experience', a process of discovery. It's not about the dissemination of answers, from one group who have them to another who don't, but about finding your own answers in action. We often lack the motivation to assimilate new knowledge because things are OK, more or less, as they are and so '...ignore great bodies of experience, any clearly analysed instance of which might present us with a very real necessity for change'.[1]

All too often, we measure our progress and achievement using criteria and benchmarks designed to guarantee our success because most of what we set out to do we have done before. We are, most times, looking to validate our methods, call it all best practice and then do it all again somewhere else. It keeps us competitive and saves time. Our motivation, most times, is meeting targets and generating contracts, much less so reflection and discovery.

Lack of motivation, rather than lack of time or experience, is one of the main reasons why learning fails, at whatever level of enquiry, in addition to agency competitiveness and professional defensiveness. When experience tells us, or circumstances demand, that we need to shift our work habits or behaviour, our attitudes or methods, we become defensive rather than accommodating, and hold on to the safe ground of well-tried routines. When we do change, it is often in response to markets rather than need or new findings – to stay ahead, promote careers, safeguard the brand. Staying ahead takes precedence over staying relevant – in the short term at least. We inadvertently or otherwise deny the wisdom, intuitive know-how, tacit knowledge implicit in the routine of the everyday because it's fuzzy or messy. It lacks rigour and discipline. How could you justify or anticipate the value of buffaloes or bus stops to build community, or the unplanned yet intricate ways of building from waste?

The result is that we spend our time as experts convincing others to change their ways, or worse, we reshuffle the problems to suit the objectives we have already set ourselves, so that we can succeed! We redefine the problems we encounter in ways that enable us to exercise our competence and power – to suit what we do best and not what we need to do in response to conditions on the ground. All of this undermines motivation to learn, to change and puts a block on innovation and interrupts development.

For development practitioners, working with PEAS, reasoning backwards is fundamental to learning in action and in so doing to positioning problems in ways that unlock alternative solutions. As we have seen, when we confront a problem or opportunity on the ground during our first phase of action planning, we at first describe its characteristics and then enquire with all about its cause. I see what I see very clearly, but what am I looking at? I try to explain what is happening and why. In this way, I position the problem in ways that can lead to appropriate although sometimes unlikely responses. And so, the community who were less interested in getting the school bus into their settlement (widening and paving streets, moving houses, negotiating lot boundaries) but instead getting the kids safely out (cycle rickshaws as school buses or guided on foot, partnerships with government, local employment for 'drivers', security for children, environmentally friendly transportation). Or the demand for a new clinic (new building), which turned out to be a demand for improved access to the existing one up the road (training paramedics, mobile clinics, reserved hours for children only).

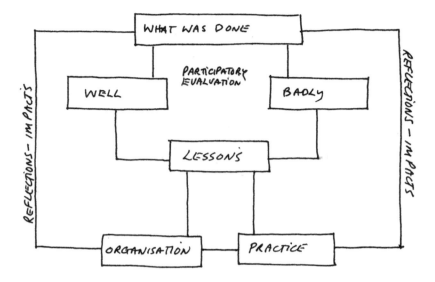

Figure 11.1   *Learning and change*
Source: Nabeel Hamdi

As we proceed in our quest to improve our practice, we are guided not just by our skill or competence, but also by our commitment to truthfulness and good work – by the logic and reasoning inherent in the actions we take[2]. In this sense, our practice is more art than science. In his book *The Craftsman*, Sennett says 'good work comes from a progressive and lifelong commitment to learning'. He goes on to suggest three activities that are fundamental in this respect: to reflect and to question; to open up; to localize. The diagram above illustrates this.

REFLECTING, OPENING UP, LOCALIZING

Learning in action at first demands that we evaluate what we did, and with others. What went well and what did not go so well, to whom and why. It is a participatory learning process in which those to whom the impact of interventions is greatest have a dominant say about its value. From these assessments and narratives we draw lessons and discuss to whom the lessons apply. Importantly, we reflect on what impact the lessons have on the way we may have to reorganize, or in the attitudes, tools, methods of practice, or on relationships between actors. And then, how will all this feed back into adjusting work this time or doing things differently next time?

The first cycle of routine – describing behaviour or what we have done, evaluating success and failure, deriving lessons, is to question and to reflect on quality and performance. It is to ask whether or not the precedents we used (not just the actions we took) from which we learnt last time are still valid – to justify taking the same actions this time. Precedents offer us a point of departure, not of conclusion or a preordained answer. This is how it was done last time, guided as it may have been culturally, technically, economically, environmentally. How can we disturb it all this time in ways that create new relationships, new meanings, better ways of conserving water and energy, safeguarding against natural disasters, for example? We improve our understanding of the way things were and are in order to move on continuously rather than discontinuously, not to replicate. Imitating precedents, even when successful, is a sure formula for failure because time and circumstances are bound to have changed.

Learning from precedence is not, therefore, a nostalgic response to the past, or about defending the current situation. Neither is it a negligence of history, when old precedents no longer apply, when history can no longer explain unprecedented or discontinuous change of today, and when new precedents need to be invented. In unprecedented times, when need and meanings change, so then does the history from which 'now' derives. In this way, our work and our projects join the continuum of history in placemaking, informing generations, not just bureaucrats. This contribution to the library of precedents is 'the most solid source of adult self-respect' and reward.[3]

The second cycle of routines – working from the impact of lessons on practice or organization, back to the differences these will make on implementation, on behaviour, before the cycle is then repeated, continuously – is about opening up and about localizing.

Localizing, in practice, means making things concrete and relevant to the conditions we encounter in the street – giving definition to local needs and aspirations and, at the same time, making global policies locally specific – for example, the MDGs or agreements on climate change initiatives. Local agenda 21s are a good example, as are the lessons now well articulated on participatory planning that today find a variety of interpretations suited to local conditions. In this sense, localizing ensures ownership, of both problems and solutions.

In the context of learning, opening up is about expanding the value of small interventions and of new precedents, and ensuring their impacts are widely felt. Opening up ensures that new precedents become integral to the knowledge of agencies, a part of their institutional memory.

There are, however, a number of barriers to localizing and to opening up. Many of these we have already explored: dependency-inducing behaviour provoked through over-specialization; the ubiquitous gaps between practice and policy, theory and practice and the dominance of global themes and international agendas over local ones; the pervasiveness of forward planning intent on localizing, but not always contextualizing, global themes. The 'collaborative learning project' points out that many communities '...complain about how "the donors" agendas which are usually driven by political agendas set in donor country capitals ... affect decisions about outcomes of international aid efforts, without regard to the real situations and local priorities in their area'.[4]

A further set of barriers are imposed when the medium of dissemination is inappropriate – when communication is interrupted, particularly in our dialogue with local partners and community groups.

COMMUNICATION AND LEGIBILITY

'Most agencies think they know more than communities do, and what they are interested in may not match community priorities. For example, a [donor agency] programme brought cheese to the Samburo (a nomadic tribe) area to increase the protein in their diet because that was a sign of development [to the donor], and people melted it like ghee and put it on their skin to protect them from the sun instead.'[5]

In thinking through the design and delivery of learning programmes we need first to decide the purpose of learning and the dissemination of lessons learnt. Is it to change behaviour, to persuade or to inform? Is it intended to stimulate thinking in search of creative alternatives to solve problems, or is it to change attitudes or shift paradigms? Each intention will demand differences in media and in process. All, however, will need to avoid pre-emptive prioritizing or pre-packaged answers.

As we can see from the example above, people were not motivated to accept the diet of cheese because protein was not a priority for them! Motivation to engage, to understand, to learn must be mutual and, in all respects, a basis to participatory learning.

Other times, when working with communities, people will lack the motivation to learn because the place of learning is unfamiliar, because the medium or iconography is culturally or otherwise abstract, or because the language used is demeaning or illegible. This lack of legibility inhibits participation in learning, whether in fieldwork or class work. People wind up being lectured about things that don't interest them much. Learning becomes passive. And 'when dialogue becomes monologue, oppression ensues'; power relations are reinforced.

Legibility takes on many forms and is a vital part of ensuring that lessons learnt are localized and that they therefore make a difference. There are various ways of thinking about legibility, all of which will influence the ability to learn, to assimilate learning into the cultural practices of communities and organizations and the ability to participate in the learning process.[6]

Social legibility is about differentiating between social groups who we know will assimilate and interpret information in different ways. Age, gender, ethnicity, class, caste, income or vulnerability will all be significant in this respect. Our inability or unwillingness to differentiate in order to include, because we lack time or access to marginal or minority groups, may exclude precisely those whom we set out to include because they don't turn up, or, if they do, they don't participate. In these ways, we might privilege those who are already privileged in however small a way, despite the good intent. 'What is clear is that attention needs to be paid to issues of difference and the challenge of inclusion.'[7]

We also know that acceptability of lessons learnt will be determined partly by patterns of patronage, trust or influence. Familiarity of context will also influence receptiveness to new knowledge and new ideas, as will the status of facilitators who may not locally '...correspond with any understood model or social relationship'.[8] In social settings where hierarchy is respected, presenting an opinion may be seen as a sign of dissent, even disrespect toward leaders, elders or officials. 'Someone who is voluble and assertive in one setting may be silenced in another. Someone looked up to with respect in one's sphere may find themselves patronized and even derided in another. The mutual impingement of relations of power and difference within and across different arenas, conditions possibilities for agency and voice'[9] as it does the value and purpose of learning.

Language and media of expression is key to cultural legibility, as are pride, suspicions and aspirations. Prevalent belief systems will place significant differences on the value of information or routine. Methods such as gaming, role play and theatre will lack professional credibility for some, or may demand relationships among actors that are unfamiliar or unacceptable. Books, posters, maps or sophisticated diagrams may similarly block rather than facilitate access to knowledge and information. Technologies, with all their implied difference in behaviour and process, may not fit the needs, desires or expectations of people, whatever their practical advantage. On the other hand, modern or 'respectable' imagery, although sometimes unfamiliar, may be more acceptable because it represents progress – what could be in the future, rather than what is now.

Legibility also demands transparency, the opportunity to see through the implications of any change or habit or livelihoods, should it be pursued. In participatory work, this means knowing the gains and losses of adopting, for example, new standards or construction, or restrictions of trading, or new habits in the use and storage of water – so that informed dialogue can take place.

Recently, I witnessed one man who asked an official who was explaining his plans for their settlement after upgrading, what the blue patches were, in which he had noticed his own house was located. The official told him that his area, zoned blue, was not for commercial use. He would have to close his shop, which was adjoining his house. It would reduce pollution, avoid congestion, increase safety, he was told, lessons we have learnt from analysis of a variety of projects nationwide. Hard choice, replied the man, between a healthier environment (which he did not believe) and the loss of livelihood!

Transparency entails agreeing criteria for evaluating trade-offs – of health, safety, affordability – ensuring that these are understood and fit for purpose and that they are negotiable. Clear maps, jargon-free language, as well as the use of the local vernacular are key. While some may well understand bus stops as communication models or roads as lines of primary communication or even rooms as geometrically configured spaces, others will not!

Graphic and visual legibility is key in all respects. Diagrams, cartoons, speech bubbles, sectional drawings, zoning maps, may be familiar media of expression for one party (urban communities, for example) but not to others. Diagrammatic abstraction can be easily misunderstood, as can abstraction in 3D models.[10]

In my work in London, we had made at first a large model that families could use to plan their homes. The model had a grid of grooves in its wooden base, into which wall panels could be slotted, arranged and rearranged to divide up rooms. Balsa wood block of various sizes were provided which people had to imagine as beds, chairs, TV sets and other bits of furniture. Communication with families was difficult. No one could figure out why they were going to get grooved floors, and what that would mean when laying carpets! Neither were the abstract blocks understood – they lacked the personality of real furniture. We architects were all about function and much less about display and status, which was of greater concern to families.

In another participatory workshop in the arid landscape of southern Sudan, one well-intentioned facilitator was explaining to his community the relationship between root causes of problems and their symptoms or manifestations. He had displayed on the wall a chart with four 'problem trees'. In the absence of trees in their landscape and, for some who may not have seen a tree of the kind displayed, the symbolism was illegible. For many, it looked like the foreign consultants were proposing to plant a forest of trees, which, in view of their other urgent needs, was kind, if somewhat puzzling!

Then there was the consultant who talked about achievement and the need for courage in order to reach their goals. He was showing them cartoons of a man climbing a mountain and celebrating when he had reached the summit. For the assembled community, sitting in the wake of a recently active volcano, his achievement to them was an example of stupidity rather than courage!

And when a cartoon of a house with eyes and legs and a speaking face was shown to communities in Pakistan, an example of safe houses in earthquake prone areas, the eyes were thought to be electricity meters and the mouth a boat. The idea of a house that was alive and happy was incomprehensible.

Clarity on who the target population is, is essential information, literal representation is all-important to clear graphic legibility.

12

REDUCING DEPENDENCY, CULTIVATING OWNERSHIP

In this chapter, we return to a fundamental theme in the debate on lasting change, on targeting primary causes of problems and the discontinuity of programmes: ownership and dependency. In Chapter 8 on PEAS, we reviewed the dependency-inducing practices of providing as a discrete expert routine. We observed the coercive objectivity of its reasoning, its propensity to decide on issues and on interventions from the top down and from outside in, or its tendency toward charity. 'This assumed objectivity is founded on implicit principles of division, hierarchy and exclusion – principles through which scientific research can turn into an excellent agent of control'[1] and, therefore, dependency. Neither does giving induce ownership. Ownership comes from an ownership of process, of problem and of solution. I have constantly seen and heard well-intended experts, NGOs and others decide on a problem, legitimate maybe but not perceived as a problem by community, and, if so, certainly not a priority. People will go along with what outsiders say or have decided because, in the process, they may just get something worthwhile for themselves, which in their lives of least expectation is better than nothing. Worse still, the poor will then get handed the responsibilities to implement priorities decided by others – what Banargee and Duflo call 'mandated empowerment'.[2] That is, the inevitability of having to do it themselves, albeit with a bit of help, on the assumption that by doing so, they will in time come to own it.

Two other causes of dependency are important to note because they give context to practice at both the micro and macro levels:

the first, the dependency that comes with aid, especially tied aid; the second, dependency induced (sometimes inadvertently) by the wrong choice of technology.

In Chapter 1, we tracked selectively the history of development that from the start tied the economic and sometimes social activities of 'recipient' or 'beneficiary' nations to the interests of 'donors'. It was Richard Nixon who in 1968 said, 'let us remember that the main purpose of American aid is not to help other nations but to help ourselves'.[3] This axis of superiority and inferiority between nations and communities, north and south, embedded still in the language of development, perpetuates dependency and inequity, however charitable the motives:

> ...charitable conditionally structures the poor out of decision-making by defining them as beneficiaries in the worst sense of the term. Taking this to the micro level, Ngunjiri argued that most participatory development begins by stigmatising local communities as having a 'problem' as opposed to seeing communities endowed with many positive assets. The strong forces that push people and their communities into accepting their weak and impotent location, are fundamental driving forces in shaping relationships and partnerships with the development organization that works with them. Dependency rather than empowerment is the inevitable outcome.[4]

At the micro level, there are calls for aid to be targeted more at improving relations on trade in the fight against poverty. The assumption here is that targeting aid to building trade capacity in partner countries will not only reduce poverty but will also move them from a state of dependency to one of interdependency. Pascal Lamy, Director General of the World Trade Organization (WTO), suggests that the move away from the aid or trade debate to one of 'how to deliver gains from both' is the surest way to sustainable economic development. In this way, more of the US$10 million worth of international trade a minute can be shared with the poorest countries, which currently account for only 0.4 per cent of this trade, half of what it was in 1980.[5]

Giles Boulting argues for related policies in this respect.[6] The first, Aid for Trade, or building trade-related capacities, means reforming taxes, improving import and export processes, meeting international health and safety standards. It also means improving the economic infrastructure of partner countries (transportation, roads, energy, communications). The second encourages Economic Partnership_Agreements. These are regional agreements between the European Union (EU) and African, Caribbean and Pacific Countries (ACP). Thirty-five ACP countries are currently signed up that can export to the EU and are protected from EU competition at home.

In both the above cases, reforming international trade rules to allow better access to the markets of rich countries and reducing subsidies that make EU and US goods and produce more competitive than local ones, will be key. While developing countries 'comprise roughly three-quarters of the WTO membership' and while the aim to raise trade capacity funding among major donors, improve transparency and reflect better the development dimension of trade in WTO rules (Doha Development Agenda 2001) is worthy – real change in relationships and results on the ground have yet to be measured.[7]

Conspiracy theory suggests that development through trade is another version of trickle-down theory. And that aid will be directed even more into trade liberalization in order to exploit markets in developing countries. Ladislau Dowbor provides us with a stark example from Guinea-Bissau of the dependencies of tied aid and the perils of the market, in particular when it is left unregulated.

> ...The Dutch company HVA had the equipment of a large sugar production plant for sale. They sent a technical team to Bissau, which quickly produced three thick volumes showing that the country needed a sugar plant of exactly this size, even though it was absurdly over-sized. They informed the Minister of Agriculture that HVA had sufficient influence in the Dutch Government to obtain financing for the plant in the form of International Aid, if the Government formally requested the plant from them. With the request in hand, HVA would then pressure 'friendly' members of the Dutch Government, using time-honoured mechanisms, and Holland would end up providing aid of X millions to Guinea-Bissau – not to meet the country's most pressing needs, of course, but to buy the Dutch equipment. This is called 'tied-aid'. Guinea gets

a white elephant whose chronic deficits will be a permanent drag on the
public accounts. The money never leaves Holland because it is simply
transferred to HVA. HVA keeps the profit from the operation. The Dutch
Government gets votes by publicizing its generous help to poor countries.
Dutch taxpayers foot the bill, along with the people of Guinea, who will
have to support yet another ill-considered 'development' project.[8]

Mansour Ali further illustrates the short-comings of dependency
induced by the wrong technologies, especially when tied to aid, in
his observation recently of 'gift aid'. Mansour tells his own story:

During my past work in waste management, I saw a number of cases
of inappropriate technologies gifted as aid and almost lost the excitement
of hearing more, because as the story starts – I immediately know the
ending. I developed my own constructs and biases on things which
are said and things which are obvious but neither said, nor discussed.
However, the interesting thing is that this situation will continue – the
story of sending inappropriate technologies and external specialists with
big ideas, good intentions but less time. The only difference I observed
this time is that this orthodoxy is proliferating with more money and
longer duration programmes, leading to larger failures.

Gedarif has had a twinning programme with a municipality in
the Netherlands since 2000. This is a long-term programme, focusing
on improving waste management in Gedarif. The programme has
carried out feasibility studies, baseline studies, set up a self-fee payment
mechanism and trained the staff through exchange visits to European
countries. The programme also funded health education and community
education. I was told that 40,000 'women' have received training on
waste management because women play an important role in this respect.
These software inputs were smartly linked with the hardware inputs
of supplying one truck per year. The programme somehow concluded
that since Gedarif has wide streets, a suitable option is house-to-house
collection using large compactor vehicles of 18 tonnes/trip. The house-
to-house collection is considered as the most expensive type of collection
system and 18 tonnes is the heaviest and perhaps the largest vehicle in
use in Europe. In addition, a number of studies have concluded that
compactors are not the best trucks to handle heavy and dusty waste,
a common condition in low-income countries. These trucks also need
expensive spare parts and special workshops for repair and maintenance.

On top of it all, these trucks were second hand. In return for this gift, a number of changes were made in policies, legislation and practices of Gedarif state. Even hospitals and clinics started separating infectious and non-infectious waste. There was a target meeting operational costs through charging fees by the year 2005; and then comes the interesting part of the story.

The trucks were soon requiring spare parts, maintenance etc. They were also found 'not suitable' for the unpaved roads, especially when they are fully loaded. Municipalities also discovered that when it rains, the trucks were inoperable as they are designed for paved and well-kerbed roads of European cities. So, quickly, a mechanical engineer was sent to look into these issues. S/he suggested that the Gedarif municipality needed a proper workshop and a full complement of spare parts, to be supplied from the Netherlands. This is now happening. They also suggested wheelie containers (which are only usable on paved surfaces!). By 2014, Gedarif would have electricity from the landfill gas, so it was argued: 'but our waste is dry and we need a lot of water to make sure that anaerobic digestion happens' was the final comment from the head of waste management in Gedarif.

The international development sector is full of such sad and true stories and this is another. Despite the good intentions of the Dutch public and their municipal officers to help Sudan and the efforts of Sudanese officers, the programme has neither benefited the environment nor the people of Gedarif. [9]

Tied aid, inappropriate technologies, the kind of forward reasoning that often shuffles the problem to fit the solutions already devised, and the resulting lack of ownership, are all systemic to the dependency that development can induce, without the corrective of reasoning backwards.

13

BUILDING LIVELIHOODS

In Part II of this book, we explored a number of interventions designed to improve the physical and economic life of Thawra to make it a destination, a wonderful place to grow up in. To each of our catalyst interventions, we made space for the strategic objective of building and sustaining livelihoods of individual households and of the community at large. We were directed in our pursuits by current wisdom, to tackle poverty. That is: in order to reduce poverty, one needs to reduce vulnerability in all its manifestations, as we have elaborated in Chapter 3. Reducing or removing vulnerability, in turn, demands building the resilience of community, to the shocks and stresses of daily life, the capacity to safeguard and sustain livelihoods, 'the ability to cope, adapt and improve well-being...'[1]

Significant in this respect is the ability of the poor to access essential resources, not just to meet basic needs, but in doing so to accumulate and safeguard capital assets – natural, financial, human, physical, social and political. Texts on livelihoods and Department for International Development (DfID's) sustainable livelihood model are plenty;[2] I will not attempt to repeat or summarize these here. There are, however, a number of characteristics that are an important part of our reasoning in Action Planning and a key part of the process of making practice strategic.

There are two things to highlight: first, the theoretical importance of livelihoods to the understanding of poverty and, in particular, urban poverty; second, the implications of these theories in practice. I will use David Sanderson's version of the sustainable livelihoods framework, the simplest and clearest, in my view, among all the other overly complex interpretations that I have seen.

PEAS and its underlying rationale of reasoning backwards are consistent with the livelihoods framework in that its starting point is the household. As Beall and Nazneen Kanji argue in their theme paper to ESCOR '...policy will be more effective and equitable if it begins with an understanding of household level strategies and uses a livelihoods systems framework to understand the linkages between smaller units such as households and communities and the larger-scale economic social and political processes operating in and on cities'.[3]

Definitions of livelihood vary in detail rather than in substance. For example, livelihoods 'comprise the capabilities, assets and activities required for a means of living'. Another definition emphasizes 'resilience' as integral to understanding livelihood strategies: 'Livelihoods are the mix of individual and household survival strategies developed over a given period of time that seek to mobilize available resources and opportunities.'[4] In all cases, livelihoods are seen as more than people's productive lives but also how people gain access to resources and their relation to the wider economy.[5] They include both a practical and a strategic understanding of how poor people acquire and also contribute their assets to improving their own well-being and the well-being of cities. This, despite 'the myth of marginality' still associated with the poor.

The sustainable livelihoods framework has been widely interpreted and applied by DfID, CARE, Habitat for Humanity and many others across a broad range of programmes. It is useful for analysing people's assets and, importantly, makes explicit the asset opportunities implicit or latent in place and in project design.

For example, I know what a house *is*, but what does it *do* to acquire skills, improve health, ensure security, build wealth, and all kinds of social and political capital? I know what a standpipe *is*, but what does it *do* to generate income, empower women, improve health, build community? If we apply the same questioning to buffaloes, mushrooms, homestays and all the other interventions we had contemplated in Thawra, we begin to draw a very different and more explicit map of the sometimes hidden potential and then opportunity of all our interventions, from the point of view of livelihoods and the well-being of people.

Criticism has recently been levelled at the Sustainable Livelihoods Framework in various ways. It is mostly associated with small scale projects where the focus now in response to the Poverty Reduction Strategy Papers is on national policy; that it doesn't offer an effective way of analysing power relations, nor all the social exclusion associated with poverty; that the framework is too open and not easy to measure in its effectiveness, so far as reducing vulnerability; neither is it able 'to deal with issues beyond the local economy, such as national development and international trade';[6] that it doesn't deal with rights or governance; that it is different things to different people and not easy to pin down.

It is worth recalling that our understanding of livelihoods has derived from our progressive and deeper understanding of the dynamics of poverty and in response to the 'multi-dimensionality of the experience of poverty'.[7] It has emerged in response to an approach to poverty that, at one time, 'chiefly measured income or consumption and focused solely on outcomes'. It moves us on from looking only at productive processes to looking also at consumption and social relations in securing livelihoods. It moves us on to considering the value of interventions in building assets, not just solving problems. David's road map is useful in all these respects.

Its strength lies in its simplicity and in its narrative style. It is grounded on the fundamentals of livelihoods as processes already in place, not something invented by experts. Sustainable livelihoods approaches are used, more as a route map than as an overt programming tool; they describe how things are (and point to how things should be) rather than tell you what to do. Used holistically, they respond easily to most of the critique levelled so far.

At the centre is the household[8] that, in order to meet its basic needs, needs access to essential resources. Basic needs include food, water, shelter to safeguard health and well-being, but can also include security, dignity or other intangibles. Essential resources may include land, materials, money and also health facilities, knowledge and information, education. Two questions are immediately evident: the first, what blocks access to resources? The second, who controls resources? The first is about discrimination, the second is about

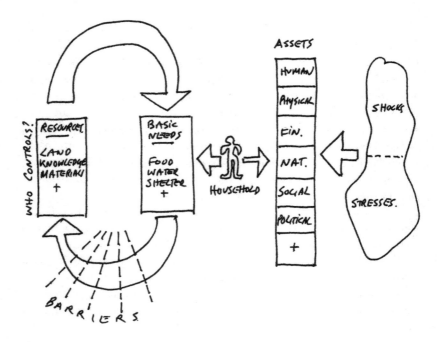

Figure 13.1   *Sandersons's livelihood framework*
Source: Adapted from David Sanderson

power relations. Both are further barriers to achieving the strategic value of practical interventions.

In the first case discrimination of whatever kind is often built into the customs, laws and standards that we apply. You can't get a loan without collateral guarantees; you can't vote without a title to land; you can't go to school without a uniform. At a macro scale, exclusion from markets, trade agreements are all forms of discrimination and impact households, directly or indirectly.

Power relations in so far as who controls resources are varied. Who decides who has access to clinics or clean water? Who controls land markets? Who has a monopoly on materials? Power relations are played out locally – the selling of water, for example, from one family to others, who may not have legitimacy, the control on land by the self-appointed, in community landlords or speculators.

Power relations are, of course, also played out city-wide, nationally and globally – all of which, again, impact households.

Managing constraints, removing barriers, facilitating access to resources and moderating power relations are a dominant part of the rights agenda. The livelihoods approach and the rights agendas, therefore, coincide around the management of needs and of resources. Few poor households, however, are able to accumulate assets for the longer term. This inability to accumulate assets leads to chronic poverty, the kind we explored in Chapter 3, and to the intergenerational transfer of poverty. Rickshaw drivers in Dhaka, for example, use up their labours and face many difficulties in old age. Children are often required to look after the elderly and are, therefore, denied education and so on. All of which renders the poor vulnerable to shocks and stress.

Stresses, as we know, are daily and recurring: the insecurity of jobs or land tenure, political insecurity, the uncertainty of getting your children to school, or of accessing your local clinic on account of your ethnicity. Shocks, albeit more intense or momentary, often induce long-term impacts; the shock of losing your job or the illness or death of the principal household earner; natural disasters or conflict, for example.

Most of us will have accumulated safety nets in response to shocks and stresses in the form of assets. Carol Rakodi provides us with an excellent outline of household capital assets and how we might go about increasing and safeguarding assets. Natural assets, for example, include land for cultivation and readily available materials, livestock. Physical capital includes basic infrastructure, productive equipment, housing. Then there are financial assets, including savings, remittances and pensions. Human assets include labour available to the household, as well as the skills and expertise that households may acquire or which might be inhibited by the lack of educational opportunity or the demands of household maintenance. Social capital often refers to the social networks that people build and, therefore, their mutual reliance in case of emergency or need. Political capital is about one's ability to voice one's needs, and more to engage in the governance of place – to be able to influence decisions that affect your well-being.

If we now reflect back to our project at Thawra we can begin to see and document, using Sanderson's road map, what difference all the interventions can make to livelihoods and well-being. The social capital we built in the process of mapping where people learnt more about themselves and each other; the alliance that emerged from that and all the other events – theatre, music, mural making and thought trees. We can begin to map and make explicit the social, physical, financial and natural capital that began to accumulate around Betty and mushrooms. The physical capital that was built through what became known as The Knowledge and Enterprise Centre, the urban farm and community enterprise facility; the social, human and financial capital emerging from the furniture recycling workshops, the added financial capital from homestays. Importantly, the beginnings of connecting household livelihood with the wider economy, nationally, even globally, through their unlikely partnership with the Ministry of Tourism, through the 'Home Depot' type of outlets and even the global fair trade movement. Then there was the political capital and engagement with good governance promoted through the community-based organizations – the alley and cluster communities, for example. And with all of this, the building of security through an agreement on land tenure, the raising of dignity and self-esteem of ordinary people, their sense of place and belonging.

In all these respects placing livelihoods in the centre of our research for building community ensures a better synergy between people and place, needs and aspirations, and between solving problems and changing worlds.

PART IV
TEACHING

The good teacher imparts a satisfying explanation; the great teacher, unsettles, bequeaths disquiet, invites argument.

Richard Sennett

REFLECTION:
THE MESS OF PRACTICE

My training as a development practitioner taught me to be respectful, participatory proactive, consultative, humble, diplomatic and polite. At work I discovered I had to be direct, blunt, decisive, laid back when necessary, arrogant and authoritative. As a student I was taught how to deal with complex situations through role-play and simulation. At work I played multiple roles, as an NGO consultant voicing survivors' needs, as a UN expert advising government, as an international consultant with pretence to confidence and as a woman who was also from a developing country. At the end of stressful day in field work, I would ask myself what if anything I had achieved dealing with all the challenges, mostly unforeseen and playing all those roles for real.

My first assignment was in Aceh in Indonesia helping to rebuild houses for tsunami survivors. This was a liberating experience working with a large expatriate group of colleagues from all kinds of backgrounds. For my first professional project I had authority and enjoyed being in at the start. I avoided diplomacy, I said what I thought, I believed I was right and felt good about the difference I was making.

When I arrived in Pakistan, where I spent 18 months with an NGO helping in the reconstruction of 600,000 houses after the earthquake, my first impression was that there were no women anywhere in public, and if there were, for example waiting for buses, they would be sitting on the ground and hiding, like a rock under their dark burkhas. In Pakistan I stayed in 15 different places – guesthouses, tents and hotels. I was stared at all the time; I was subject to dodgy phone calls day and night. During my telephone interview for this job I assured my interviewer that I understood the culture of the place given, after all, that I was from nearby Bangladesh. But in my first week after arrival I realised how wrong I was.

My second shock was from colleagues in the international NGO office, who were surprised (even shocked) to see a small, young woman who didn't look like an ex pat, but acted like one. Then there was the hassle of keeping my distance and respecting boundaries. A male colleague, obviously wanting to check me out, offered to go out for a drink with me in an Islamic State. Knocks on my hotel door in the middle of the night. Meetings arranged in field tents at 10 at night without consideration for female colleagues — how do I get there, who takes me back. Support staff not listening to you, because you're a woman — endless small stresses. Later I learnt how to cope. Not being too friendly or nice, but being demanding, authoritative and loud instead. Choosing my battles to fight on issues and accepting the ways things are, against my better judgement.

My third professional shift, also in Pakistan, was with the UN. I was responsible for overseeing housing construction and for training army personnel and government officers in one of remotest districts in Kashmir, where according to estimates 35,000 houses were damaged. My staff was largely male and trained as engineers, there were few others with whom I could socialize. Here I found the primary objective of some colleagues working for the UN was not to save the world, but status and careers. For me working in this position enabled me to establish my authority, particularly with the army and the government with whom I was working.

The reason I continue to work in the development field despite all the social and professional challenges is to build capacity and enable others, which I find most rewarding. Recently when I went back to Pakistan it was encouraging to see how my field office which I had left two years previously with five staff and a car now had a full national team of 50 staff with 13 cars and a successful programme. What I have learnt is that every effort no matter how insignificant contributes to the greater cause and that teamwork and perseverance is everything. I have also learnt that so many who think they are saving the world are often not professionally competent to do so and that in any case it's important to save yourself before saving others. In spite of the fact that trust is such an important part of our relationship to people I learnt in Pakistan that it's better to trust your own instincts and intuitions.

Importantly I learnt not to let the practicalities of today interfere with the ideas of tomorrow.

Rumana Kabir

14

THE INTERVENTIONS STUDIO

Poverty, social and political exclusion, inappropriate technologies, environmental degradation, conflict and natural disasters all contribute to accentuating vulnerability and risk.

This studio will explore what it takes to design an appropriate response to shelter and settlement upgrading – inclusive, secure, adaptive, sustainable – for a settlement in Bangkok, Thailand. We will develop the skills and competencies which designers and planners need in order to respond effectively to situations that are extreme, where vulnerability and risk are endemic. Under these circumstances, resources are often limited or inaccessible, demand is urgent and uncertainty a way of life. Working under these extreme conditions requires new ways of thinking, new tools and techniques, new methods, new partnerships. It demands new kinds of creativity at once practical, strategic and artistic, grounded in a fundamental commitment to the humanitarian agenda of rights and social justice.

How do, or how should these commitments and ideals shape design thinking and practice? How do they shape decisions on the built environment? What roles and responsibilities are required for designers, planners and others? What skills, values and competencies do they demand? What form of housing, what materials, techniques, technologies are appropriate to the longer term building of community?

So reads the introduction to the design studio that I have run with colleagues at the Development Planning Unit, University College London (UCL) and have done with variations at Oxford Brookes University and at the Rhode Island School of Design (RISD) in Providence, USA. While at Brookes, the students are undergraduates and entirely architects, at RISD and DPU they are graduates and also include landscape architects, engineers, industrial designers, planners, art historians, anthropologists and more. We locate ourselves wherever the issues are dominant, sometimes in actuality when we start with field-based work, sometimes by way of simulation and role play in class. Our context recently was Bangkok, an informal settlement similar to one explored in Part II. The learning opportunities and objectives of fieldwork differ in obvious ways from class work.

Both are equally significant for teaching and learning, for reasons I will elaborate on later in this chapter. Our focus for now is on class work. The privilege of class work is that you can become engaged, without becoming encumbered. It enables you to step out, in order to reflect, before you step back in.

I do not have an elaborate pedagogic theory that drives my teaching, only common sense, empathy with the student dream, whatever it is, and a shared ambition to 'rehearse the future'. I try to craft a path somewhere between the realities of the world as it is (which we need to know and understand, although not always to accept) and the one we hope it could be – to liberate our imagination, invent new realities, to dream a bit. Taking risks, changing roles, disturbing the professional *status quo* are all important in these respects. I tell the class that this is probably the only chance you have to get something wrong, or wind up in an intellectual blind alley, and still get an 'A' grade – assuming, of course, you are rigorous about your failure!

At the start, we are clear in our learning objectives, which we work out together, but less clear about outcomes, preferring these to emerge in doing. In this way, teaching can respond to individual student needs and educational expectations as they search for meaning and method and, at the same time, contribute to building our collective knowledge out of individual discovery. From the start, I nurture that dynamic relationship between individual ambitions and collective effort, in the importance we therefore attach to teamwork, usually assumed to mean everyone doing everything together all the time.

In all these respects, the learning environment we cultivate is free and associative. That is, free to explore issues and individual routines, as you stumble upon them and in whatever medium is appropriate; and associative in the constantly shifting relationships with colleagues and staff – their ideals, ideas, values, meaning and interpretation. For this reason, we structure the programme using scenarios or narrative written by student groups based on their understanding of place and people, rather than overly prescriptive 'design briefs' or programmes that have a tendency also to stereotype. A house, a school, a street or notions of public or private to someone from Kampala is different from someone from Liverpool!

As the 'Architects for Change Guide to Supporting Student Diversity' (2006) suggests: 'schools and teachers [of architecture] need to be aware of the impact of staff values, priorities and unexamined stereotypical assumptions on the cultural commentary they provide. This is particularly so where teaching staff and visiting lecturers are predominantly homogonous in terms of gender, ethnicity, social and cultural background.'[1]

As we socialize our differences and understanding in class, so each one of us will change in order to fit, to join the consensus on issues, but without losing individual identity. In all these respects, the class is an 'exemplar' of practice.

The programme of class work, over the three months or so of term time, is structured broadly into seven linked phases of work:

1   A short one-week exercise, designed to explore PEAS and get everyone talking – not just listening.
2   A simulated street walk, as if on site – an outsider's view, reasoning forwards.
3   Profiling livelihoods, needs and aspiration – the insider's view, reasoning backwards.
4   Invading the site and agreeing on guidelines for development – community directed, outsider facilitated.
5   Planning the site – insiders and outsiders.
6   Detailed design of selected projects/programmes.
7   Building a prototype.

In our first introductions, we probe into each others' motives for joining this programme, for engaging with development, before we discuss our learning objectives. What are our aspirations? Over the years, I have distinguished, broadly, three different groups of students and young professionals who want also to become development practitioners.

The first group includes those who love their architecture or engineering and who want to continue in their profession of choice but in a way that is relevant to some of the big issues that they have they decided are no longer just someone else's problem – social justice, climate, poverty. They want to place themselves in settings that challenge their disciplinary conventions and, in so doing, to become more skilled and competent at what they do in a way that is connected, rather than to do something else.

The second group want to change careers, either because they can no longer associate with the values and priorities of their existing ones, or because they have achieved their stage of incompetence, or just because they have got bored. They want 'to give something back' and do good in a world that they see as full of injustice. For teaching, I find this group the most challenging and, potentially, the most rewarding. Firstly because their search for new meanings and relevance demands a more open and indeterminate discussion of purpose and learning outcomes, difficult in an academic climate that demands both to be explicit upfront. As anyone searching for a career will know, you cannot be certain what you need to learn because you are not sure what you want to do or be until you find out! Discussion on these issues is usually highly productive, with questions raised in respect of purpose, of every opinion or class routine. Secondly, the desire to do good brings with it strong values and big commitments. While they may not have made up their minds about learning objectives, they have usually done so about good guys and bad guys, where to lay the blame for all the injustices, about the way the world should be. As such, this group is clear on positions and offers a good platform of values and ethics, of judgement and opinion for others to challenge. For teaching, the question is how to encourage positions, but in ways that are open for colleagues to disturb.

The third group of students who join development are somewhere in transition between the first two. They come more curious than committed, looking for change – for a while at least – which, who knows, may lead to better opportunity. They are often attracted by field trips to faraway places that they may never otherwise visit, or by the need for another degree and preferably from one of those prestigious institutes. Overall, this group tends to be younger, more glib, with jargon of development, more liberated by their ignorance. They care less about the rules or constraints imposed by reality, however it is delivered, which in any case most have yet to confront. They are arguably, therefore, readier to take intellectual risks and be more creative in their design work.

All three groups, in different ways, share an aspiration to become engaged in ways that define and reward rather than consume. I am who I was and who I want to be, and not just whom *they* say I am or should be. In this sense, all three groups had become sceptical of 'normative nowhere man' after years of formal education – a diet of rigour that had distanced them from relevance. All three could see the 'professional or career cul-de-sac' to which their disciplinary education was leading.[2]

The dynamic between all three groupings offers a creative setting for learning and teaching, as does the interdisciplinary and often multicultural mix of people.

LEARNING OBJECTIVES

When it comes to learning objectives, we brainstorm in groups what we want to learn or find out about, as a measure of self-progress throughout the academic year. I will have my own list, as I am required to do, derived from teaching in previous years, and also from the demands that will be placed on each in practice. There will, therefore, be significant coincidence between their objectives and mine. A typical set might read as follows:

- develop skills and competencies related to PEAS (mine);
- understand participatory processes, methods and techniques including negotiation, consensus building and conflict resolution skills;

- raise awareness of the social and rights agendas and look to ways in which they will discipline architecture, planning, engineering or whatever you are or want to be;
- explore alternative presentation and communication skills to suit a variety of cultural settings, formal and informal, literate and non-literate;
- understand concepts of community
- explore relationships between Insiders and Outsiders and what each brings to planning and design, working through gatekeepers;
- working in societies divided by class, income or ethnicity – on the edge of conflict;
- build a concept of ethical practice;
- learn to work in disciplinary and interdisciplinary teams;
- cultivate flexibility and entrepreneurship (mine);
- self-care (mine).

Some of these objectives are clearly better explored in field work (divided societies, gatekeepers, insider/outsider relationships) in the knowledge that however much we role play in class, the realities of class will always be neater, more ordered, more controlled than the realities in the field.

In concluding our introductory sessions, I adopt three overriding ambitions for students: first, the importance of the practitioner as an activist – not the kind you find in street demonstrations or hugging trees, but someone who gets things going, looks for chance, challenges rules, rejects constraints, gets involved, takes risks – in order to bring about positive change.[3] Someone who does and by reflection knows. Becoming wise, as an activist, is as important as becoming competent.

Second, to be wise and competent, to be effective as an agent of change, you have to have moved on from that stage of dependence on conventions and routines and also from that stage of independence, seeking star status that sets you apart from colleagues, where your differences count more than your effectiveness, to that stage of interdependence – the sociable expert, sharing not hording knowledge, learning from colleagues and community, seeing the positive in other people's ideas and ideals, looking for the best case and not worst case in your opponents' arguments.

Both of the above feed my third ambition for students, whatever their own: that is to reinvent themselves professionally and, eventually, to be able to articulate with example what that might mean for each, individually. In that sense, at the end of the term, I get everyone to take a stab at rewriting their own code of conduct.

Finally, I present my own wisdoms or code of conduct from *Small Change* to guide the learning process throughout the term, to become activists and interdependent.[4]

> *Ignorance is liberating*
>> *Start where you can: never say can't*
>>> *Imagine first: reason later*
>>>> *Be reflective: waste time*
>>>>> *Embrace serendipity: get muddled*
>>>>>> *Play games, serious games*
>>>>>>> *Challenge consensus*
>>>>>>>> *Look for multipliers*
>>>>>>>>> *Work backwards: move forwards*
>>>>>>>>>> *Have fun, feel good*

EXPLORING PEAS

We start work, Phase 1, with a short intensive (one week) exercise in randomly mixed groups, designed to socialize the group and get everyone thinking about PEAS. It introduces the idea of a catalyst intervention and the practitioners as activists and engages everyone with ordinary people. Its purpose is to generate discussion *in action* from the start, about some of the key themes of the term – find out gaps in knowledge and expertise and inform me about the kind of additional lectures or seminars we may need throughout the term. Interventions are left to each group to decide with one requirement: it must be in the public realm – in a street, a square, the university yard and it must attract and engage with the interests of the public.

Examples are various, as are responses: the transformation of the exterior of the DPU on Tavistock Square, designed to stop passers-by and to inform them about what went on inside; the potted plants in Euston Square to socialize an unsociable public space and engage with people, mostly transient, about their sense of place; the invasion of the university courtyard at Brookes – a shelter built from recycled materials which became a tea shop for students and a place for smokers in between lectures. It competed with the university franchise for catering and invoked complaints from campus planners – it was illegal and untidy and had not had the approval necessary from health and safety. It was as if a metaphor, designed to invoke all the conflict and constraints that come with informality or illegally invading land – a catalyst with which to

Figure 14.1   *Catalyst intervention, Oxford Brookes University design studio*
Source: David Sanderson

engage with users and authorities about rights, the private use of public space and more.

In all cases, we began a discussion on each of the four components of PEAS: what did you provide? What (in this exercise) did it enable you or others to do? What changes would it inspire or demand, to rules, regulations, or the perception of people about values, ownership or belonging? And then, if you were to keep these initiatives going, if not the installations themselves, how would it all be sustained? What did it take to engage people's interests, how did you lead into your dialogue, who took the initiative? What more would you need to provide now, soon or later?

STREETWALK

After a week, we were ready to contemplate our site. We divided into groups of professional teams (our first role play) appointed by their client of choice: the Ministry of Tourism, the World Bank, an international NGO – all outsiders of community and some of country, doing their pre-feasibility mission. The task here was to simulate a site visit, identify key issues with respect to each team's mandate and expertise converging, where possible, local needs and global agendas agreed in Paris, Washington or Rio.

First, the country context and urban setting was profiled, the site introduced together with related issues of access and tenure. At the DPU, Supitcha Tovavich (my teaching assistant from Thailand) played the role of the local planning authority and made the presentation. We then 'walked the site' – using slides. As we did, we encountered many of its features, characteristics and issues – pirated electricity, piles of garbage on waste land, historic buildings, all kinds of creativity and innovation with waste materials to build shelter, to grow vegetables. We asked each group to respond to two questions: I see what I see very clearly but what am I looking at? And, in respect to materials, public open spaces, playgrounds in various states of repair or disrepair, we asked: this is what it is – but what could it become, and with what kind of help?

We made a 1:200 scale map of the site, which fills the classroom floor and piled on our perceptions and findings – cut-outs and Post-it notes collaged with not too much detail at this stage. The output here was a draft log framework analysis – reasoned forwards from purpose derived from the bigger and outside agendas – MDGs for example or from the values or mandate of each organization, then localized with objectives, activities and possible outputs – a quick first response.

PROFILING LIVELIHOODS

In Week 5 we shifted gear and regrouped. Each group (now consisting of one person from each of the previous professional groups, more or less) took on the role of a local special interest group, a community-based organization whose focus may be in women's rights, employment, children or other minorities. Each group profiled its assets, needs, hopes and vulnerabilities. It was an insider's view of how things worked, of quality of life and well-being. The objective: to develop a set of community derived guidelines for the upgrade of the site and the settlement of the adjacent site, which will have to be negotiated between groups. Each group appointed a representative – a higher level CBO to develop the guidelines. We encouraged each group to immerse themselves as best they could in a role play, in the life of place and to present their profiles in whatever medium – for radio interview, TV documentary, artistic installation (thought trees, murals), posters or cartoons.

Everyone also built a scaled model, from materials from waste bins, of their ideal house in order to discuss their family needs and aspirations to support livelihoods, or shelter extended families, for example.

INVADING THE SITE

At about Week 8, we invaded the site with our ideal houses and ideas for public space and other facilities. The objectives here were to consolidate the guidelines derived through the profiling exercise and also to drive home the need, albeit in simulation, for community organizing. There would be conflicts of interest among interest groups, not everyone would have the space they needed on site, nor would their priorities necessarily match. During the exercise, students familiarized themselves, as a part of their learning objectives, with tools and techniques for troubleshooting, consensus building and negotiation. These were all sub routines, facilitated by two or three students nominated to act as outside facilitators.

The invasion of the site could take many forms, either real or modelled. At the Eden Project, for example, during one of our Architecture Sans Frontières (ASF) annual summer schools, participants were not made aware of a real site, which we had identified for occupation, in the wake of one of Grimshaw's bio-domes. Each participant made a drawing of their ideal home, free to decide on space, needs and utilities, and to think about materials. When it came to the invasion, and when participants discovered that to fit everyone on to the site, together with access and some minimal public space for children's play, they would have to halve, at least, the size of their homes. Negotiations were intense, of who would get what and where and how much. There were tussles over location and land grabs. It wasn't long before everyone agreed that each group would nominate a representative, to sit on a CBO and negotiate. Creative ideas emerged for better use of space and for more efficiency of effort. Communal kitchens, for example: shops at the commercial edge of the site cooperatively owned for trading and commerce. And not everyone needed to collect everything for building: some collected and fetched card, others bottles, others wood and so on. A tool chest was established (there was one hammer, two saws, bundles of wire, some nails and so on) and managed by another community group to safeguard equity. The whole was built from Eden's waste-neutral centre. Everyone spent a night in the makeshift settlement and cooked the evening meal, to experience the cold, the lack of privacy, the density, the vulnerability (the overnight stay was illegal), the neighbourliness and the newly discovered interdependence among all.

San's Story

My name is San.
I'm 13 years old.
I live in a garbage mountain.

My mum is 33 years old.
She sews the clothes for the factory
at home from morning to night.

For lack of light in the evening,
she has gradually lost her sight.

My father is alcoholic. He is 38 years
old. Since he lost his job 6 years ago,
he is drunk every day.

Now he left but sometimes he
comes back for money.

Figure 14.2   *Family profiles BUDD student work at the DPU*
Source: Roi Kavalieratou, Hui-Chen Liu and Dharshana Thibbouwawa

My brother is only 5.
My mum takes care of him in
the morning.

I look after him in the evening.

In the day time, I go to a
morning-market for collecting
remnants.

On the way home, I collect tins and
cans from some restaurants.

They know me very well and
those areas are mine.

In the night time, I carry my small
truck to a night market for more trash.
I also walk to the city to get some
clean water.

When I go back to my house, my mum cooks and cleans our room.

It is my turn to take care of my brother. I like to use the garbage to make a toy for my brother.

I do my laundry in the river.

I help my brother to take a shower by using the precious clean water.

A toilet is located in the outside of my house.

When I was young, I was terrified to go there when it is dark.

Now I get used to it.

In the raining season, it rains a lot.

There was a huge flood 2 years ago and my dog was drowned.

Collecting trash on the streets is dangerous because one of my friends lost his leg by car accident.

I wish...
I wish that I have a larger space to collect more garbage and sell it to recycling enterprise.

I wish that we could live in a comfortable and safe house.

I wish my mum will stop working and focus on taking care of my brother.

I wish my father won't hurt us any more.

Is that too much to ask?

Figure 14.3   *Dream house model BUDD student work at the DPU*
Source: Supitcha Tovivich

Figure 14.4   *Invading the site, Eden Build, ASF Summer School*
Source: Supitcha Tovivich

Figure 14.5   *Building components from waste and recycled materials, Eden Build, ASF Summer School*
Source: Rachel Hamdi

In class, we had no such privilege. We used the same scaled plans on which we had done our mapping as professional teams and now overlaid these with our models, similar to Patama's planning in Bangkok for the Under the Bridge Dwellers.

Importantly, the whole group, through negotiations, had developed a set of rudimentary guidelines for setbacks, building height, privacy, street widths and communal spaces. There were other guidelines for markets, for a recycling enterprise centre, children's play, urban farming – and yet others for how the water's edge would be used.

PLANNING THE SITE

In Week 9, we regrouped into expert teams, as interdisciplinary as we could get it – architects, planners, engineers appointed (as if)

Figure 14.6   *Invading the site with models – BUDD student work at the DPU*

Source: Supitcha Tovivich

Figure 14.7 *Deriving community guidelines for site planning, Bangkok*
Source: Patama Roonrakwit

by the government, in agreement with their donors, to begin the planning process. Each team now consisted of one member from each of the community groups. The priority here was to decide a plan of action, based on the guidelines generated by community, modified, however, to ensure compliance with the demands of the local planning authority. The site was, after all, a part of larger urban setting, and there were responsibilities beyond the specifics of this location. Each group was guided by the PEAS framework, in its search for strategy, interpreted by each group as needed. Each group was required to make explicit lessons learnt from good practice about housing design, site planning, infrastructure planning, and how these lessons would modify or be modified by the community's guidelines.

In these ways, each group was confronted with having what they thought was best practice, modified to less than best by needs on the ground and vice versa. We came to learn of the difficulties

A framework for intervention (for example: housing)

Strategic	Practical					
	Land/zoning	Ownership/tenure	Finance	Technology	Construction/ Implementation	Etc.
Change — Now						
Change — Soon						
Change — Later						
Constraints						
Primary causes						
Livelihoods/ poverty						
Scale — Local						
Scale — Urban						
Scale — Regional/national						

Figure 14.8   *Practical work and strategic work: a framework for interventions*

Source: Nabeel Hamdi

we experienced professionally, the discomfort we felt when what we knew was good practice was challenged and modified by what was appropriate and do-able. The results were a series of strategic interventions (for site planning, community organization, technology development, enterprise building, urban farming) with enough details to judge feasibility but not too much to distract from principles. We coupled with these practical interventions a short exercise (one day) of what it would take to implement and also the changes it would demand in thinking or practice or standards, the constraints that would have to be overcome, the primary cause of some of the problems that the interventions would have to target.

DETAIL DESIGN

Around Week 12, each student selected a component of the larger plan to develop in detail – a catalyst to get it all going and also working toward a shared vision of how it could be soon or later.

For this detailed phase of individual work, I offered the following framework of questions that would need to be answered:

- What will you do?
- Why will you do it?
- How will you go about it?
- What will you produce?
- How will you measure progress or success?
- What assumptions or risks do you anticipate?
- How will you safeguard against these?

Examples of detailed projects could include a house or components of a house designed to be adaptable; prefabricating building components from waste and the social enterprise it would initiate; a 'shelter box' for emergency use; a mobile help van for self-builders; a training kit; an 'edible place' for children's play with playgrounds and equipment to enjoy and, at the same time, to inform on waste recycling and plant cultivation.

BUILDING A PROTOTYPE

In the last phase of work, everyone built a prototype of their detailed design, which could take many forms. Some would be in model form, others full scale. At the DPU, our students visited CAT (Centre for Alternative Technology) in Wales where they had a chance to build full scale, from local material. Others, who had been exploring non-physical interventions – 'social' enterprise in urban farming, for example – would develop a prototypical scenario, which they could test out with colleagues. The importance of making a prototype is twofold. First, it is a vehicle with which to engage others – an interactive way of exploring options, for housing or play – a tool with which to communicate or demonstrate opportunities latent in waste. Second, it is another level of enquiry into your design, 'learning from touch'.[5] In either case, and whether scaled or full size, prototypes transcend representation. They are a part of the placemaker's tool kit, as we witnessed in Part II.

Figure 14.9   *Detail design–house kits studio project at Oxford Brookes University*

Source: Supitcha Tovivich

Figure 14.10   *Building prototypes – the living wall.*
ASF Summer School at Eden

Source: Rachel Hamdi

FIELDWORK

Not all learning objectives can, of course, be met effectively in class work (self-care, gatekeepers, working in divided societies). There is no substitute for field work (in the same way as there is no substitute for class work) and most programmes I know couple fieldwork to class work. There are also numerous examples of studio work that is substantially field based including, for example, the Rural Studio started by Samuel Mockbee at Auburn University in the early 1990s, or Chalmers University's Reality Studio, a full semester field-based programme with the University of Nairobi.

At Brookes, with Centre for Development and Emergency Practice (CENDEP) students, we would regularly start Semester 2, in January, in the field – a two-week self-contained programme working with communities in partnership with our host NGO Community Architects for Shelter and Environment (CASE), for example, or ACHR and our counterpart a local university.[6] This programme of visits and hands-on work leads sometimes to more detailed work back in class. At the DPU, our students spend a month in the field after class work is done trying out field methods, including participatory techniques, engaging with issues none of which is as neatly programmed or sequenced as they are in class.

Most importantly, perhaps, in fieldwork, one learns to work in messes, to cope with disappointment, with achieving results you know are less than best, with people who are intent on getting in your way, with timetables that don't work and meetings that never happen.

The MIT student reflections below are revealing in these and other respects. The first two from our work in Dakshanpuri in Delhi (4–14 January 1994); the second from our workshop in Belfast (28 January–9 February 1996) that took place just before the IRA bombings in London.

> *The globalization of architectural training and practice leads to a general indifference to delicate social issues and dilemmas. Coming from a former British colony, I cannot ignore events in our colonial past that had seminal influence on the way in which architectural education has*

developed in this region. The architectural curricula and the pedagogical framework, despite an apparent political gloss, systematically alienate the students from the socio-political realities of the region. The design exercises in the architectural schools generally revolve around some dominance assumptions that seldom bridge the training and the social needs. The Dakshinpuri experience, perhaps, deepened my scepticism over the ability of traditional training of architects to address the present social realities.

Adnan Morshed, Delhi 1994[7]

Our intent was to learn through doing, and our action plan involved conducting rapid appraisal methods to identify problem areas and opportunities for improving community life for the squatter settlement in Dakshinpuri. In particular, we set out to conduct a rapid reconnaissance of the key issues within the community, get feedback from community members on our findings, engage in further field research and inquiry into specific problem areas, and finally, present our recommendations to the community and influential institutions.

While we had a plan of action, we soon realised that our ability to implement it would not be entirely within our control. There was a prevailing sense of uncertainty each day about what the particular logistical circumstances of the moment would allow us to do. An unpredictable assortment of activities took form: fleeting group gatherings, prolonged waits, ad hoc interviews and data collection, and intense bursts of preparatory activity for presentations ... Amidst this bewildering environment, I found that my engrained conditioning in thorough and systematic inquiry became almost an impediment to action. Efforts to engage in concerted planning and coordination inevitably seemed to disintegrate each time. Instead, spontaneous, impromptu decision-making and action became the mode of group interaction. I came to realise that rapid adaptation to these new rules became the key to being an effective player.

Karen Khor, Delhi 1994[8]

Wednesday February 7th 1996
Good day yesterday. Met with Kevin, a community activist who we've been dealing with for the past week, to discuss plans for the RUC [Royal Ulster Constabulary] barracks. Kevin lives right across the street from

the barracks and to make it even more interesting, he is a devout Socialist (bust of Lenin on his TV table) and an IRA man who has spent time in Portolaoise Goal. He was fascinating to talk to, though he wasn't able to give much advice about funding. He took us on a walk around the site and up the hills to get a view of it. We soon became aware that we were being followed/monitored by a helicopter, which make us very nervous about taking photos, despite Kevin's assurances. Coming down, half a dozen RUC Rovers passed us and entered the barracks and then we heard a loud report, which called all of us to attention as, thinking at first that it was a gunshot, we jumped about 3ft in the air.

Friday February 9th 1996

I am so frustrated and angry. Yes, it was going slowly and painfully but we were closer to peace than we have been in 25 years – perhaps than we have ever been. It kills me to think that I may have been with people this week who knew this was going to happen. I hate that my first reaction was 'I'm glad I am leaving tomorrow.' I feel like I'm running away. The barricades and checkpoints are back already. The RUC are wearing flak jackets and the army maybe here by the morning. We hope that there will be no rioting or revenge killings tonight, but we have no reason to have confidence in that. I could not walk tomorrow to the places I walked today and for the last two weeks, and know that I was safe. All the work that we, and the communities and many others have done over the past 18 months may be lost, back to square one. Gerry Adams won't get one more concession without decommissioning. Clinton may get crucified for this. When we got here few people had confidence in the peace process, and we had no faith that anything would change. By Thursday, a lot of us, including some we worked with in the community had hopes. Now there is just sadness, frustration and despair. I can't put an up note on this. Right now, everything feels impossible, that they will never learn to live together. I hope I am wrong but how can you have confidence in that when the city is at war again.

Catherine Preston, Belfast[9]

15

THE PLACEMAKER'S CODE

In conclusion, I suggest three levels on which to reflect, progressively and continuously. The first, a reality check, as we reflect again on the larger context of constraints, however you select them, in order to maintain engagement and sustain responsibility. I see these, therefore, as a context for work, in the short term at least, not a barrier to it. I offer below my own selection and summary. Second, we need to reflect on seemingly contradictory expert roles and practice routines, but which are importantly complementary. Third, I invite everyone to write their own code of conduct, for which I offer a number of preliminary headings to get you going. These, I would hope, will become a progressively adaptable part of the placemaker's toolkit.

THE CONTEXT OF CONSTRAINTS

There will always be inevitable contradictions in development objectives, between the moral duty to ensure safety and equity in all sectors of work, and the economic drive for growth. There will be the social and humanitarian agenda of rights, the desire to moderate or even eliminate discrimination, to reduce vulnerability and promote social inclusion; at the same time, the political incentive to govern, to allocate resources often for political expediency more than for social well-being. We know that cities will continue to grow with a shift in migration patterns increasingly from city to city, rather than rural to urban; and that the form of cities will continue to be market or demand driven, determined largely by individuals and organizations with power in money or political clout, and less by planning or by civil society, however much participation; that the ability of governments to govern will continue to be limited, because their mandate to do so is never conclusive; that there will always be resource constraints, however much aid in money or expertise; that the poor have a limited capacity to pay for services and utilities and that some form of subsidy is inevitable in the foreseeable future, as are less conventional partnerships for supply and management; that standards we know to be safe and equitable, for building, services or utilities, will largely be unaffordable, in particular if we continue to invest in one-off, time-bound interventions; that most urban institutions will have a limited capacity to implement big plans and that these will, therefore, have to be worked toward incrementally and adaptively; similarly, that urban institutions, in whatever sector, will have a limited capacity to enforce regulations or control the tide of informality. The informal sector in most cities of the south will continue, therefore, to predominate.

We now recognize that there will always be limitations to community participation and good governance, given the networked rather than place-based structure of community in cities, and given the persistence of unequal power relations and corruption locally, nationally and globally.

Overall, the conclusion of our efforts to reduce or eradicate poverty is pessimistic. The poor or indigenous communities will always be seen to stand in the way of access to raw materials, despite the talk of rights. Poverty is likely to increase as a result of continued growth-oriented policies, promoted by governments and monetary institutions, and the gap between rich and poor will grow, not diminish; palliative economics, however generous, (easing the pain of economic misery) will continue to take precedence over development economics (where poor countries create wealth of their own) and that mainstream economics will continue, therefore, to focus on the symptoms or effects of poverty rather than its root causes; the MDGs are also biased in favour of dealing with symptoms rather than with the need for structural change.[1] In all these respects systems of dependency described as 'welfare colonialism' continue unabated. Aid comes with conditions attached, more implicit than explicit in today's agreements.

Lastly, lives and livelihoods will increasingly be threatened by natural disasters induced by climate change, given the densities of cities, the occupation of marginal land or flood plains and the stress of poverty on the environment; and 'the only way to meet the demands of increasing population is to intensify the exploitation of nature', while recognizing, at the same time, that nature and natural resources are themselves under threat from increasing populations...

THE COMPLEMENTARITY OF OPPOSITES

Engaging these complex themes through practical interventions on the ground will demand, as we have seen, expanding the mandate of practice beyond conventional disciplinary boundaries. In the old days, practice meant being practical, solving problems, putting up buildings, installing infrastructure, dealing with contractors. Today, and as I have argued throughout this book, responsible practice must assume strategic objectives as well: inducing change, dealing with primary causes of problems – not just symptoms – cultivating choice, scaling up programmes, managing constraints, dealing with the kind of global issues illustrated above that can no longer be relegated to 'others', whatever your discipline. Practice, in this context, is as much about triggering novelty and making things happen as it is about solving problems.

A number of additional things to think about and reflect upon in this respect, all clustered around seemingly contradictory but, in fact, complementary objectives. The first is more of a reminder: to plan forwards, inclusively and effectively it's best to reason backwards. As I hope to have already demonstrated, unravelling the policy implication of what is already going on on the ground, whether successful or not, is a good way of informing policy from daily practices, so that policy and practice are convergent rather than divergent in their purpose.

Second, also a reminder: that the best way of scaling up the impact of projects is to scale down the size of units or organization, of management and decision making to make sure that accountability is held locally and that success or failure is measured by those who are affected most. Scaling up then is about federating or networking lots of small relatively autonomous units of organizations (network governance) and not about making entities bigger. Scaling up and scaling down are complementary practices.

Third, as we put things together whether a building, a place or a programme, as we construct our projects, so at the same time we must deconstruct the underlying purpose and process and so make it all accessible and transferable. Making the invisible more visible, demystifying decision making, avoiding the jargon of expert routines is both a moral obligation and an ethical responsibility of practice.

Deconstructing practice invites community to influence both process and outcome. It is the ethos of the sociable expert. Constructing projects and deconstructing practices are complementary processes.

Fourth, when we engage the mess of the everyday, we invoke both order and disorder; the order of habit and routine with all their clearly defined rules, rituals and laws implicit in culture and context; and the 'disorder of progress',[2] one that disturbs rather than disrupts, as we decide our interventions. The disorder of progress proceeds, usually in increments and often randomly, as we stumble upon opportunity and good ideas. Each step in planning tells something about the next steps, as we reason backwards from effect to cause, to objectives to purpose. This, after all, is one of the driving principles of action planning in its attempt to engage with the creative and adaptive mess of informality. In our search for structure, we distinguish between the hidden order of mess (chaos theory) in order to tap its ingenuity and then disturb it where necessary, and the absence of order – the reality of 'mess'. 'Most messes encountered in daily life are failed orders, someone had an organizing scheme in mind but, for one reason or another, it didn't work.'[3] Our housing estates and master plans with their bias toward neatness are often failed orders 'struggling to fight off randomness'.[4] The order of place and the disorder of progress are complementary processes.

Fifth, there are the tensions between the need for divergence, to explore avenues of thought that may lead to new practices and to be inclusive of differences, and the demand for convergence, of interests and priorities in order to reach decisions. Too much divergence can lead to chaos, even conflict; too much convergence normalizes differences and usually in the interests of those who can shout loudest. It leads to lowest common denominator plans and designs, suitable for everyone in general but no one in particular. The balance, therefore, between divergence and convergence is delicate and constantly changing. Divergence and convergence are complementary routines.

Finally, there is the ubiquitous and seemingly irreconcilable contradiction in objectives, faced by all professionals, between the need to be rigorous and disciplined according to the norms set out by academics and professional bodies and the imperative to be relevant to the global issues that we all now confront. I do not believe that these two positions are inherently contradictory. They are, in fact, complementary. The question is, how to be rigorous in a way that is relevant? In this sense, the way we think to work must combine both agendas, left and right, in the diagram below.

THE WAY WE THINK TO WORK

RIGOUR	RELEVANCE
REDUCTIVE	EXPANSIVE
CERTAIN/CONSISTENCY/PRECISE	UNCERTAIN/UNSTABLE/AMBIGUOUS
LITERAL/EXPLICIT	METAPHOR/IMAGERY/NARRATIVE
SERIAL THINKING	ASSOCIATIVE/HOLISTIC/SYSTEMIC
GENERIC/PROTOTYPICAL/ABSTRACT	PARTICULAR/CONTEXTUAL
EXPLICIT KNOWLEDGE	IMPLICIT KNOW-HOW
SYSTEMIC, FROM BOOKS	IDIOSYNCRATIC, FROM PLACE
PREDETERMINED	SERENDIPITOUS
KNOWING/DATA HUNGRY	OPTIMAL IGNORANCE

Figure 15.1 *Rigour and relevance: the way we think to work*
Source: Nabeel Hamdi

REFLECTING ON CONDUCT

The third area of reflection is about our own code of conduct as professionals. I invite everyone to reflect on the contents of this book and on the beliefs and values that underpin their practices and to sketch out their own code of conduct geared, as it must be, to the ambitions they hold for themselves individually and for humanity collectively. I offer the following tentative headings below to get everyone going...

Figure 15.2 *Development practice and the placemaker's code*
Source: Nabeel Hamdi

NOTES AND REFERENCES

GENERAL NOTE

I have quoted from the following of my previous publications throughout the book:

Hamdi, Nabeel (1991) *Housing Without Houses* Van Nostrand Reinhold, New York and Practical Action Publishing (1995), Rugby

Hamdi, Nabeel and Goethert, Reinhard (1997) *Action Planning for Cities: A Guide to Community Practice* John Wiley & Sons, Chichester

Hamdi, Nabeel (2004) *Small Change: About the Art of Practice and the Limits of Planning in Cities* Earthscan, London

See also my chapter entitled 'Learning and Dissemination' in Gandelsonas Catalina (ed.) (1999) *Communicating for Development: Experience in the Urban Environment*, ITDG Publishing, Rugby

PROLOGUE

1. See for example *Architectural Design* (AD), Vol. XLIII 11/1973, special issue entitled Housing/Flexibility
2. These projects were widely reported in all of the major architectural journals. See for example *OAP, Journal for the Built Environment*, Vol. 34, No. 8, August 1971; *RIBA Journal*, Vol. 78, No. 10, October 1971; *Building*, Vol. CCXXIV, No. 6787, issue 26; *Design 275*, November 1971; *AD Special Issue: Pick of the Projects*, Vol. XLIV 5/1974
3. See *Architects Journal*, Vol. 171, No. 9, 1980

CHAPTER 1

1. Joe Perkins (2007) 'Searchers, Not Planners', *London Review of Books*, Vol. 29, No. 11, London

2. See Rod Burgess, Maria Carmona and Theo Kolstee (1997) 'Contemporary Spatial Strategies and Urban Policies in Developing Countries: a critical review', in Rod Burgess, Maria Carmona and Theo Kolstee (1997) *The Challenge of Sustainable Cities* Zed Books, London

3. Marie Huchzermeyer (2004) *Unlawful Occupation: Informal Settlements and Urban Policy in South Africa and Brazil* Africa World Press, Trenton, NJ

4. Wheaton, William C. (1983) 'Housing Policies in Developing Countries', *Openhouse*, Vol. 8, No. 4

5. See Rod Burgess, Maria Carmona and Theo Kolstee (1997) 'Contemporary Spatial Strategies and Urban Policies in Developing Countries: a critical review', in Rod Burgess, Maria Carmona and Theo Kolstee (1997) *The Challenge of Sustainable Cities* Zed Books, London

6. Marie Huchzermeyer (2004) *Unlawful Occupation: Informal Settlements and Urban Policy in South Africa and Brazil* Africa World Press, Trenton, NJ

7. Michael C. Cohen (1983) 'The Challenge of Replicability', *Openhouse*, Vol. 8, No. 4

8. Michael C. Cohen (1983) 'The Challenge of Replicability', *Openhouse*, Vol. 8, No. 4

9. Michael C. Cohen (1983) 'The Challenge of Replicability', *Openhouse*, Vol. 8, No. 4

10. Peattie, Lisa (1982) 'Some Second Thoughts on Sites and Services', *Habitat International*, Vol. 6, No. 1

11. Hamdi, Nabeel (1991) *Housing Without Houses* Van Nostrand Reinhold, New York and Practical Action Publishing (paperback, 1995), Rugby

12. UN-Habitat (1987) *Global Report on Human Shelter* UN Human Settlements Programme, Nairobi, Kenya

13. Michael C. Cohen (1983) 'The Challenge of Replicability', *Openhouse*, Vol. 8, No. 4

14. See Rod Burgess, Maria Carmona and Theo Kolstee (1997) 'Contemporary Spatial Strategies and Urban Policies in Developing Countries: a critical review', in Rod Burgess, Maria Carmona and Theo Kolstee (1997) *The Challenge of Sustainable Cities* Zed Books, London

15. Marie Huchzermeyer (2004) *Unlawful Occupation: Informal Settlements and Urban Policy in South Africa and Brazil* Africa World Press, Trenton, NJ

16. McGillivray, M. and Clarke., M (eds) (2006) *Understanding Human Well-being* UN University Press, New York

17. Asian Coalition for Housing Rights (2008) 'Community Finance: the news from Asia and Africa. Report of a Workshop held in November 2007', Poverty Reduction in Urban Areas Series Working Paper 19, International Institute for Environment and Development (IIED), London

18. Caminos, H. and Goethert, R. (1978) *The Urbanisation Primer*, MIT Press Cambridge, MA

19. Hanley, Lynsey (2008) *Estates: An Initimate History* Granta Books, London

20. Schrijvers, Joke (1993) *The Violence of Development* International Books, Utrecht

21. Schrijvers, Joke (1993) *The Violence of Development* International Books, Utrecht

22. Schrijvers, Joke (1993) *The Violence of Development* International Books, Utrecht

23. For overviews of the NHDA, Sri Lanka Million Houses Programme see Sirivardana, S. and Lankatilleke, L. (1988) 'Some Key Issues in the Participatory Planning and Management of the Urban Low-Income Housing Process', National Housing Development Authority (NHDA), Ministry of Local Government Housing and Construction, Colombo, Sri Lanka. Also, for case studies see Goethert, R. and Hamdi, N. (1988) *Making Microplanning: A Community Based Process in Programming and Development* Practical Action Publications, Rugby

24. Browne, Stephen (2007) *Aid and Influence: Do Donors Help or Hinder?* Earthscan, London

25. See the *Guardian*, 1 September 2006, p.29

26. For an overview of these two themes, see *Ontrac*, the Newsletter of International NGO Training and Research Centre (INTRAC), no 33, May 2006

27. For an overview of these two themes, see *Ontrac*, the Newsletter of INTRAC, No. 33, May 2006

28. Joe Perkins (2007) 'Searchers, Not Planners', *London Review of Books*, Vol. 29, No. 11, London

29. UN-Habitat (1987) *Global Report on Human Shelter* UN Human Settlements Programme, Nairobi, Kenya

PART I INTRODUCTION

1. *Impact Measurement and Accountability in Emergencies: The Good Enough Guide* (2007), Oxfam Publications, Oxford

CHAPTER 2

1. Thawra is an imaginary place, but which is typical of most slums and informal settlements. It represents a composite of different places I have worked in and researched.
2. See Diana Mitlin (2008) 'Urban Poor Funds: development by the people for the people', Poverty Reduction in Urban Areas Series, Working Paper 18, IIED, London
3. Dowbor, Ladislau (2005) *The Broken Mosaic: For an Economics Beyond Equations* Zed Books, London
4. Dowbor, Ladislau (2005) *The Broken Mosaic: For an Economics Beyond Equations* Zed Books, London
5. Sennett, Richard (2008) *The Craftsman* Allen Lane, London
6. 'It's hard to believe that this is what's melting the glaciers', *The New York Times* (in the *Observer*) 26 April 2009
7. Quoted in Hanley, Lynsey (2008) *Estates: An Initimate History* Granta Books, London
8. Gamage, Nandasiri (ed) (1998) *Real Voices in Development* Women's Bank Publication, Colombo
9. Sennett, Richard (2008) *The Craftsman* Allen Lane, London
10. See Marilyn Taylor, 'Transforming Disadvantaged Places: effective strategies for places and people', for the Joseph Rowntree Foundation, available at www.jrf.org.uk (last accessed July 2008)
11. Robbins E. (2008) 'Rethinking Public Space: a new lexicon for design', *Urbani izziv letnik*, 19, Stevilka 2: 18–26/140–146
12. Caminos, H. and Goethert, R. (1978) *The Urbanization Primer* MIT Press, Cambridge, MA
13. Stretton, Hugh (1978) *Urban Planning in Rich and Poor Countries* Oxford University Press, Oxford
14. Sennett, Richard (2008) *The Craftsman* Allen Lane, London
15. Sennett, Richard (2008) *The Craftsman* Allen Lane, London
16. The methods used and case examples from Sri Lanka are documented in Goethert, R. and Hamdi, N. (1988) *Making Microplanning: A*

Community Based Process in Programming and Development Practical Action Publications, Rugby

17. Gamage, Nandasiri (ed) (1998) Real Voices in Development Women's Bank Publication, Colombo

18. Based on interviews and discussion undertaken in Colombo, Sri Lank in February 2008 and as reported in *Housing by People*, newsletter of the Asian Coalition for Housing Rights (ACHR), No. 17, November 2007

19. For a full analysis of the micro finance initiatives see Mitlin, Diana (2008) 'Urban Poor Funds: development by the people for the people', Poverty Reduction in Urban Areas Series, Working Paper 18, IIED, London

20. Gamage, Nandasiri (ed) (1998) *Real Voices in Development* Women's Bank Publication, Colombo

21. Dowbor, Ladislau (2005) *The Broken Mosaic: For an Economics Beyond Equations*, Zed Books, London, p.63. See also 'Transforming Disadvantaged Places: effective strategies for places and people', Marilyn Taylor for the Joseph Rowntree Foundation, available at www.jrf.org.uk (last accessed July 2008)

CHAPTER 3

1. David Satterthwaite (2007) 'Streets Ahead: more than half of the world's people will soon live in cities', in the *Guardian*, 17 January 2007

2. See Idzi Insights (2008) *Climate Change and Cities* Institute of Development Studies, Sussex

3. See 'Redressing Risks to Cities from Climate Change: an environmental or a developmental agenda?', Environment and Urbanization Brief 15, IIED, London

4. Caroline Moser (1996) quoted in Carol Rakodi's chapter 'A Livelihoods Approach – conceptual issues and definitions', Chapter 1 in *Urban Livelihoods* (2002), edited by Carol Rakodi with Tony Lloyd-Jones, Earthscan, London

5. Chambers, R. (1989) 'Vulnerability, Coping and Policy', editorial introduction in *Bulletin of the Institute of Development Studies*, Vol. 20, 2 April

6. See 'Wealth Gap Creating a Social Time Bomb', the *Guardian*, 23 October 2008

7. Sen, Amartya (2006) *Identity and Violence: The Illusion of Destiny* Allen Lane, London
8. Putnam, Robert D. (2000) *Bowling Alone: The Collapse and Revival of the American Community* Simon & Schuster, New York
9. Hamdi, Nabeel (2004) *Small Change* Earthscan, London
10. Gamage, Nandasiri (ed) (1998) *Real Voices in Development* Women's Bank Publication, Colombo
11. See for example Schrijvers, Joke (1993) *The Violence of Development* International Books, Utrecht. See also *Amnesty* Magazine, Issue 148, March/April 2008
12. In a column entitled 'World in View', *Amnesty Magazine*, issue 148, March/April 2008, p10
13. See *Environment and Urbanization*, Vol. 16, No. 2, October 2004, editor's introduction
14. Charlotte Lemanski (2004) 'A New Apartheid? The spatial implications of fear of crime in Cape Town, South Africa', *Environment and Urbanization*, Vol. 16, No. 2, October
15. 'Towards a Real-world Understanding of Less Ecologically Damaging Patters of Urban Development', *Environment and Urbanization* Brief 14, IIED, London
16. Hasan, Arif (2006) 'The Changing Landscape of Asian Cities', *Journal of Research in Architecture and Planning*, Vol. 5
17. See 'Designing the Inclusive City', Chapter 5 in *Century of the City: No Time to Lose*, Pierce, N.R. and Johnson, C.W. with Peters, F.M. (eds), The Rockefeller Foundation, New York
18. Advisory Group on Forced Evictions to the Executive Director of UN-Habitat (2007) 'Forced Evictions – towards solutions?', second report, Nairobi, Kenya
19. Advisory Group on Forced Evictions to the Executive Director of UN-Habitat (2007) 'Forced Evictions – towards solutions?', second report, Nairobi, Kenya
20. See 'Country for Sale', the *Guardian*, 26 April 2008
21. Advisory Group on Forced Evictions to the Executive Director of UN-Habitat (2007) 'Forced Evictions – towards solutions?', second report, Nairobi, Kenya

CHAPTER 4

1. See for example Diana Mitlin and John Thompson (1994) 'Participatory Tools and Methods in Urban Areas', Rapid Rural Appraisal (RRA) Notes 21, IIED, London. See also Hamdi, Nabeel and Goethert, Reinhard (1997) *Action Planning for Cities: A Guide to Community Practice* John Wiley & Sons, Chichester; 'A Practical Guide for "Planning for Real" Consultation Exercises' (1998) The Neighbourhood Initiatives Foundation, Telford, UK
2. Beaudoux, E., De Crombrugghe, G., Douxchamps, F., Gueneau, M-C., and Nieuw, M. (1994) *Supporting Development Action: From Identification to Evaluation* Macmillan Press, London

CHAPTER 5

1. Building 'positive' spaces: Isandla Institute (2007) *Sustainable Human Settlements. Development in the Context of HIV/AIDS*, Isandla Institute, Cape Town

CHAPTER 6

1. Hickey, Sam and Mohan, Giles (2007) 'Towards Participation as Transformation: critical themes and challenges', in Hickey, Sam and Mohan, Giles (2007) *Participation: From Tyranny to Transformation?* Zed Books, London
2. Rod Burgess, Maria Carmona and Theo Kolstee (1997) 'Contemporary Policies for Enablement and Participation: a critical review', in Rod Burgess, Maria Carmona and Theo Kolstee (1997) *The Challenge of Sustainable Cities* Zed Books, London
3. Arnstein, Sherry A. (1969) 'A Ladder of Citizen Participation', *Journal of the American Institute of Planners*, Vol. 45, No. 4
4. Poole, D.L. (1995) 'Partnerships Buffer and Strengthen', *Health and Social Work*, Vol. 20, No. 1
5. Gaventa, John (2007) 'Towards Participatory Governance: assessing the transformative possibilities', in Hickey, Sam and Mohan, Giles (2007) *Participation: From Tyranny to Transformation?* Zed Books, London

6. Ward, Colin (1996) *Talking to Architects* Freedom Press, London
7. Cleaver, Frances (2007) 'The Social Embeddedness of Agency and Decision-making', in Hickey, Sam and Mohan, Giles (2007) *Participation: From Tyranny to Transformation?* Zed Books, London
8. Cornwall, Andrea (2007) 'Spaces for Transformation? Reflections on issues of power and difference in participation in development', in Hickey, Sam and Mohan, Giles (2007) *Participation: From Tyranny to Transformation?* Zed Books, London
9. See Hamdi, Nabeel and Majale, Michael (2003) *Partnerships in Urban Planning: A Guide for Municipalities* ITDG Publications, Rugby
10. Hickey, S. and Mohan, G. (2004) *Particpation: From Tyranny to Transformation?*, Zed Books, London p. 93
11. Cooke, Bill (2007) 'Rules of Thumb for Participatory Change Agents', in Hickey, Sam and Mohan, Giles (2007) *Participation: From Tyranny to Transformation?* Zed Books, London
12. Warburton, Diana (2005) 'Planning, Participation', in 'The True Costs of Participation', Brief Literature Review, first draft, September. See www.involving.org
13. Varma, Pooja (2008) 'An Analysis of Community Participation: involvement of the Alliance in building community toilet blocks in Pune slums', term paper, Development Planning Unit, University College London
14–27. All quotes and references are from Sundar Burra, Sheela Patel and Thomas Kerr (2003) 'Community-designed, Built and Managed Toilet Blocks in Indian cities', *Environment and Urbanization*, Vol. 15, No. 2

CHAPTER 7

1. From the title to Chapter 5, Colin Ward (1996) *Talking to Architects* Freedom Press, London
2. The examples are based on fieldwork and interviews undertaken in the south of Sri Lanka during an assessment of post-tsunami responses to reconstruction in collaboration with the Norwegian University of Science & Technology (NTNU)
3. See Hamdi, Nabeel (2004) 'The Bus Stop: cultivating community', Chapter 7, in *Small Change* Earthscan, London

4. Nathan Straus (1945) *The Seven Myths of Housing* Alfred A. Knopf, New York

5. For an overview of current ideas in sustainable and responsible design see *Design for the Other 90%* (2007) Smithsonian, Cooper-Hewitt National Design Museum, New York

6. 'Housing Rights and Secure Tenure: A pre-requisite for housing the poor', think-piece prepared by UN-Habitat and commissioned by the Norwegian Ministry of the Environment, March 2004

7. Diana Mitlin (2008) 'Urban Poor Funds: development by the people for the people', Poverty Reduction in Urban Areas Series, Working Paper 18, IIED, London

8. Mark Napier (2006) 'Making Urban Land Markets Work for the Poor', Programme proposal to DfID, prepared for a workshop of the Board of Advisors, May 2006

9. Ruth McLeod (2001) 'Costs Associated with Accessing Legal Shelter for Low-income Groups in New Urban Developments', *Homeless International*, Coventry

10. Mark Napier (2006) 'Making Urban Land Markets Work for the Poor', Programme proposal to DfID, prepared for a workshop of the Board of Advisors, May 2006

11. Mark Napier (2006) 'Making Urban Land Markets Work for the Poor', Programme proposal to DfID, prepared for a workshop of the Board of Advisors, May 2006

12. Mark Napier (2006) 'Making Urban Land Markets Work for the Poor', Programme proposal to DfID, prepared for a workshop of the Board of Advisors, May 2006

13. Yunus, Muhammad (2000) *Banker to the Poor* The University Press Limited, Dhaka, Bangladesh

14. Diana Mitlin (2008) 'Urban Poor Funds: development by the people for the people', Poverty Reduction in Urban Areas Series, Working Paper 18, IIED, London

15. For an outline of Patama's process, see Hamdi, Nabeel (2004) *Small Change* Earthscan, London, pp.29–32

PART III INTRODUCTION

1. 'The Cascading Effects of International Agendas and Priorities', The Listening Project Issue Paper 2008, Collaborative Learning Projects, Cambridge, MA

2. 'The Cascading Effects of International Agendas and Priorities', The Listening Project Issue Paper 2008, Collaborative Learning Projects, Cambridge, MA
3. Reinert, Erik S. (2007) *How Rich Countries Got Rich...and Why Poor Countries Stay Poor* Carroll & Graf, New York
4. Dowbor, Ladislau (2005) *The Broken Mosaic: For an Economics Beyond Equations*, Zed Books, London
5. Handy, Charles (1990) *The Age of Unreason* Arrow Books, London

CHAPTER 8

1. See Richard Sennett (2008) *The Craftsman* Allen Lane, London
2. See Marilyn Taylor (2008) *Transforming Disadvantaged Places: Effective Strategies for Places and People* Joseph Rowntree Foundation, York
3. Pierce, N.R. and Johnson, C.W. with Peters, F.M. (eds) (2008) *Century of the City: No Time to Lose*, The Rockefeller Foundation, New York
4. Aneurin Bevan (5 December 1956) in a speech to the House of Commons entitled 'Weapons for Squalid and Trivial Ends', the *Guardian*, Great Speeches of the 20th Century, No.13, 2007
5. Sennett, Richard (2008) *The Craftsman* Allen Lane, London
6. Dowbor, Ladislau (2005) *The Broken Mosaic: For an Economics Beyond Equations* Zed Books, London
7. Elmore, Richard F. (1979) 'Backward Mapping: implementation research and policy decisions', in *Political Science Quarterly*, Vol. 94, No. 4
8. Elmore, Richard F. (1979) 'Backward Mapping: Implementation research and policy decisions', in *Political Science Quarterly*, Vol. 94, No. 4
9. Cees J. Hamelink in Schrijvers, Joke (1993) *The Violence of Development* International Books, Utrecht, Preface
10. Sennett, Richard (2008) *The Craftsman* Allen Lane, London
11. Illich, Ivan (1973) *Tools for Conviviality* Calder & Boyars, London
12. Illich, Ivan (1973) *Tools for Conviviality* Calder & Boyars, London
13. Sennett, Richard (2008) *The Craftsman* Allen Lane, London
14. Brandon, David (1976) *Zen in the Art of Helping* Routledge & Kegan Paul, London
15. Moyo, Dambisa (2009) *Dead Aid* Allen Lane, London
16. Brandon, David (1976) *Zen in the Art of Helping* Routledge & Kegan Paul, London

17. See Rod Burgess, Maria Carmona and Theo Kolstee (1997) 'Contemporary Policies for Enablement and Participation: a critical review', in Rod Burgess, Maria Carmona and Theo Kolstee (1997) *The Challenge of Sustainable Cities* Zed Books, London
18. Sennett, Richard (2008) *The Craftsman* Allen Lane, London
19. Habraken, N.J. (2005) *Palladio's Children* Taylor & Francis, London
20. Ward, Colin (1996) *Talking to Architects* Freedom Press, London
21. Ward, Colin (1996) *Talking to Architects* Freedom Press, London
22. UN-Habitat Global Report on Human Settlements (1987) Oxford University Press, Oxford
23. Berger, Peter L. and Neuhaus, Richard (1977) *To Empower People – The Role of Mediating Structures in Public Policy* American Enterprise Institute for Public Policy Research, Washington DC
24. Habraken, N.J. (1983) 'The Control of Complexity', *Places*, Vol. 4, No. 2
25. Schrijvers, Joke (1993) *The Violence of Development* International Books, Utrecht

CHAPTER 9

1. See Brinkerhoff, J.M. (2002) *Partnership for International Development: Rhetoric or Results?* Lynne Reinner Publishers, Boulder, Colarado. See also Hamdi, Nabeel and Majale, Michael (2003) *Partnerships in Urban Planning: A Guide for Municipalities* ITDG Publications, Rugby
2. See Brinkerhoff, J.M. (2002) *Partnership for International Development: Rhetoric or results?* Lynne Reinner Publishers, Boulder, CO
3. See Brinkerhoff, J.M. (2002) *Partnership for International Development: Rhetoric or Results?* Lynne Reinner Publishers, Boulder, CO
4. Sennett, Richard (2008) *The Craftsman* Allen Lane, London
5. Elmore, Richard F. (1979) 'Backward Mapping: implementation research and policy decisions', in *Political Science Quarterly*, Vol. 94, No. 4
6. Elmore, Richard F. (1979) 'Backward Mapping: implementation research and policy decisions', in *Political Science Quarterly*, Vol. 94, No. 4

CHAPTER 10

1. See the following, for example. Berger, P.L. and Neuhaus, R. (1977) *To Empower People – The Role of Mediating Structures in Public Policy* American Enterprise Institute for Public Policy Research, Washington D.C. Schumacher, E.F. (1973) *Small is Beautiful: A Study of Economics as if People Mattered* Abacus, London. Fishman, R. (1982) *Urban Utopia's in the 20th Century* MIT Press, Cambridge, MA. Illich, I. (1973) *Tools for Conviviality* Calder and Boyers, London. Habraken, N.J. (1972) *Supports: An Alternative to Mass Housing* Architectural Press, London

2. Alexander, Christopher (1975) *The Oregon Experiment* Oxford University Press, Oxford

3. In post-tsunami Sri Lanka, for example, according to a UN Report, 'Hambantota – the political stronghold of President Mahinda Rajapaksa – is having 3,956 more houses built than required…Kalutra, the seat of the Disaster Management Minister, has a surplus of 1,085 houses constructed…' Lanka Newspapers (www.lankanewspapers.com/news)

4. Handy, Charles (1990) *The Age of Unreason* Arrow Books, London

5. Quoted in Dowbor, Ladislau (2005) *The Broken Mosaic* Zed Books, London

6. Kaplan, A. (1996) *The Development Practitioner's Handbook* Pluto Press, London

7. For a full description of this process and workshop see 'Case 3: Urban Upgrading Pilot Project for Schweizer-Reneke, South Africa', in Hamdi, Nabeel and Goethert Reinhard (1997) *Action Planning for Cities: A Guide to Community Practice* John Wiley & Sons, Chichester

8. Recorded in Hamdi, Nabeel and Goethert Reinhard (1997) *Action Planning for Cities: A Guide to Community Practice* John Wiley & Sons, Chichester, pp.231–232

CHAPTER 11

1. Sullivan, H.S. quoted in Daniel Goleman (1997) *Vital Lies Simple Truths – The Psychology of Self-deception* Bloomsburg, London

2. Schon, D.A. (1983) *The Reflective Practioner: How Professionals Think in Action* Basic Books, New York

3. Sennett, Richard (2008) *The Craftsman* Allen Lane, London

4. 'The Cascading Effects of International Agendas and Priorities', September 2008, The Listening Project issue paper, Collaborative Learning Projects, Cambridge, MA
5. 'The Cascading Effects of International Agendas and Priorities', September 2008, The Listening Project issue paper, Collaborative Learning Projects, Cambridge, MA
6. For a full overview of learning and communication, issues, methods and techniques, see Catalina Gandelsonas (ed) (2002) *Communicating for Development* Practical Action Publications, Rugby
7. Cornwall, Andrea (2007) 'Spaces for Transformation? Reflections on issues of power and difference in participation in development', in Hickey, Sam and Mohan, Giles (2007) *Participation: From Tyranny to Transformation?* Zed Books, London
8. Dudley, Eric (1993) *The Critical Villager: Beyond Community Participation* Routledge, London
9. Cornwall, Andrea (2007) 'Spaces for Transformation? Reflections on issues of power and difference in participation in development', in Hickey, Sam and Mohan, Giles (2007) *Participation: From Tyranny to Transformation?* Zed Books, London, p.8
10. Dudley, Eric (1993) *The Critical Villager: Beyond Community Participation* Routledge, London, p.90

CHAPTER 12

1. Schrijvers, Joke (1993) *The Violence of Development* International Books, Utrecht
2. Abhijit V. Banerjee and Esther Duflo (2008) *Mandated Empowerment: Handing Anti-poverty Policy Back to the Poor?* New York Academy of Science, New York
3. Quoted in Hayter, Teresa (1981) *The Creation of World Poverty – An Alternative View to the Brandt Report* Pluto Press, London
4. Mark Waddington and Carlos Mohan (2004) 'Failing Forward: going beyond PRA and imposed forms of participation', in Hickey, Sam and Mohan, Giles (2007) *Participation: From Tyranny to Transformation?* Zed Books, London
5. 'Trading Places', reported in *Developments Issue*, Vol. 41, 2008, produced by DfID, London

6. 'Trading Places', reported in *Developments Issue*, Vol. 41, 2008, produced by DfID, London
7. 'Trading Places', reported in *Developments Issue*, Vol. 41, 2008, produced by DfID, London
8. Dowbor, Ladislau (2005) *The Broken Mosaic: For an Economics Beyond Equations* Zed Books, London
9. Dr Mansoor Ali has worked in the international development sector for more than 20 years. He specializes in waste management and currently works for Practical Action, UK, an international charity.

CHAPTER 13

1. Rakodi, Carole (2002) 'A Livelihoods Approach – conceptual issues and definitions', in Carole Rakodi with Tony Lloyd-Jones (eds) (2002) *Urban Livelihoods* Earthscan, London
2. *Urban Livelihoods*, edited by Carole Rakodi with Tony Lloyd-Jones offers an excellent primer on the subject with contributions by Mansoor Ali, Jo Beall, Nick Devas, David Sanderson, David Satterthwaite and many others. See also Caroline Moser (1997) 'Urban Social Policy and Poverty Reduction', in Rod Burgess, Maria Carmona and Theo Kolstee (1997) *The Challenge of Sustainable Cities* Zed Books, London
3. Jo Beall and Nazneen Kanji (1999) 'Households, Livelihoods and Urban Poverty', Theme Paper 3, ESCOR Commissioned Research on Urban Development, Urban Governance, Partnerships and Poverty
4. Grown, C.A. and Sebstad, J. quoted in Jo Beall and Nazneen Kanji (1999) 'Households, Livelihoods and Urban Poverty', Theme Paper 3, ESCOR Commissioned Research on Urban Development, Urban Governance, Partnerships and Poverty
5. Jo Beall and Nazneen Kanji (1999) 'Households, Livelihoods and Urban Poverty', Theme Paper 3, ESCOR Commissioned Research on Urban Development, Urban Governance, Partnerships and Poverty
6. Caroline Pinder (2008) 'Revitalizing the Sustainable Livelihoods Approach', available at www.id21.org/viewpoints. See also the critiques of Jane Clark, Diana Carney and David Sanderson on the same website.
7. Jo Beall and Nazneen Kanji (1999) 'Households, Livelihoods and Urban Poverty', Theme Paper 3, ESCOR Commissioned Research on Urban Development, Urban Governance, Partnerships and Poverty

8. For a definition of 'Household,' see Jo Beall and Nazneen Kanji (1999) 'Households, Livelihoods and Urban Poverty', Theme Paper 3, ESCOR Commissioned Research on Urban Development, Urban Governance, Partnerships and Poverty

CHAPTER 14

1. From the Commission for Architecture and the Built Environment (CABE) 'Architects for Change Guide to Supporting Student Diversity' (2006). Available at www.cebe.heacademy.ac.uk/learning/sig.equality_ architecture
2. See 'Caribbean Odyssey', the *Guardian*, 25 August 2007
3. See Kathleen Maas Weigert (1993) 'Student Activism and Pedagogy: a reciprocal relationship in development studies' (reprint series), The Joan B. Kroc Institute for International Peace Studies, University of Notre Dame, Indiana, USA
4. Hamdi, Nabeel (2004) *Small Change* Earthscan, London
5. Sennett, Richard (2008) *The Craftsman* Allen Lane, London
6. For a range of CENDEP/MIT 'Rebuilding Communities' field-based workshops see Hamdi, N. and Goethert, R. (1997) *Action Planning for Cities: A Guide to Community Practice*, John Wiley and Sons, Chichester
7. Adnan Morshed (1994) 'Reclaiming Socio Political Territory in Architectural Pedagogy', in *Essays Exploring the Role of Architect and Planner* The Dakshinpuri Workshop, New Delhi, India. Report prepared by SIGUS (Special Interest Group in Urban Settlements) at MIT (the Massachusetts Institute of Technology), Cambridge, USA
8. Karen Khor (1994) 'Architects and Planners in Low Income Settlements: agents of change or development tourists', report prepared by SIGUS at MIT, Cambridge USA
9. Catherine Preston (1996) 'Belfast: a personal journal', in *Essays Exploring the Belfast Experience* The Belfast Workshop, Northern Ireland, report prepared by SIGUS (Special Interest Group in Urban Settlements) at MIT (the Massachusetts Institute of Technology), Cambridge, USA

CHAPTER 15

1. Reinert, Erik S. (2007) *How Rich Countries Got Rich...And Why Poor Countries Stay Poor* Carroll & Graf, New York

2. Eric Abrahamson and David Freedman (2007) *A Perfect Mess: The Hidden Benefits of Disorder* Little Brown, New York
3. Eric Abrahamson and David Freedman (2007) *A Perfect Mess: The Hidden Benefits of Disorder* Little Brown, New York
4. Eric Abrahamson and David Freedman (2007) *A Perfect Mess: The Hidden Benefits of Disorder* Little Brown, New York

INDEX